The Dance Of Kundalini

Exploring the Nature of Spiritual Awakening

Featuring Master Charles Cannon, Dr Richard Moss,
David Spero and Swami Shankaracharya

David Rivers

THE DANCE OF KUNDALINI
Copyright © 2015 by David M Rivers

All rights reserved. No part of this book may be reproduced in any form or by any electronic or mechanical means including, but not limited to: Information storage, recording, photocopying, and retrieval systems or by any other means, without permission in writing from the publisher and author, except by a reviewer, who may quote brief passages in a review.

Edited by Jo-ann Langseth
Cover Design by Natasha Rivers

The Dance of Kundalini/ by David Rivers
Previously published as "The Dance of Stillness"

ISBN: 978-0-994377913

Spiritual Life – New Age Movement.
299.93

Tandava Press
www.tandavapress.com
tandavapress@gmail.com
www.tandavafoundation.com

Tandava Press

For my daughters
Zoe Isabella and Grace Maria.

Acknowledgments

First I would like to thank my beloved Mother, Irena, for *demonstrating* to me the deepest devotional love for the Divine

Thank you to my beloved wife Natasha Rivers, you are my rock, my all. This book may have arisen as an inspiration in my own heart, yet it's manifestation is the fruit of your tireless work. I can never thank you enough. You are the incarnation of the very Goddess Herself.

Many thanks to Jo-Ann Langseth for her superb editing as well as for her thoughtful feedback and encouragement, also to Maria Sam Josepher, Rosanne Parker and Tony Cartledge for their generous and enlightening editorial assistance and feedback.

Deep bows also to Erin Beard, for her invaluable assistance in transcribing these interviews with such precision and care, as well as for organizing the itinerary of my USA travels and interviews. Without her, this book would not have happened.

To the Synchronicity Dove Foundation, thank you for financially backing this book and thereby expressing faith in the *Principle* of life, over and beyond any particular personal manifestation of Life.

Deep bows to Kia Scheer, for her wonderful foreword, friendship and support.

To Master Charles Cannon I offer gratitude from the depths of my soul for making such a book possible and for the endless love, support, and patience he continues to extend towards one and all.

My heartfelt thanks to Ramakrishna-Vivekananda Center of New York for their kind assistance and permission to reprint from "*The Gosepl of Sri Ramakrishna.*."

Dedicated To Sri Ramakrishna Paramahansa

The great Master who demonstrated to us all that it's *okay* to be *God Mad* in nondual awareness *and* utterly lost in devotional love to the supreme energy of life we call Mother. You are the very essence of the Goddess Herself. It is with love that I lay this book at your lotus feet

Sri Ramakrishna

O Kāli, my Mother full of Bliss!
Enchantress of the almighty Śiva!
In Thy delirious joy Thou dancest,
   clapping Thy hands together!
Eternal One! Thou great First Cause,
   clothed in the form of the Void!
Thou wearest the moon upon Thy brow.
Where didst Thou find Thy garland of heads before the
   universe was made?
Thou art the Mover of all that move,
   and we are but Thy helpless toys;
We move alone as Thou movest us and speak as through us
   Thou speakest.
But worthless Kamalakanta says, fondly berating Thee:
Confoundress! With Thy flashing sword
Thoughtlessly Thou hast put to death my virtue and my sin alike!
   - Sri Ramakrishna

The Gospel of Sri Ramakrishna;
Copyright 1942;
Ramakrishna-Vivekananda Center of New York;
Swami Nikhilananda (tr.)

Table Of Contents

Foreword By Kia Scherr — x

Preface A Celebration Of Possibility — xiii

Introduction:
A Thing Should Be Compared, But Only Ever To Itself — 1
My Own Journey With Kundalini — 3
Prelude To The Interviews, Mystical Vision Of A Sage — 12

The Interviews

Master Charles Cannon
Introduction: Iconoclastic Modern Mystic — 15
Spontaneous Childhood Awakening — 18
Visions Of God As Mother – The Apparition — 21
Meeting The Master – Radical Expansion — 22
The Only Suffering I Ever Had Was When I Tried To Figure It Out — 24
The Path Of Guru Yoga — 25
Going Beyond The Distinction Of I And Thou — 27
The Play Of Energy Manifests Through Our Concepts — 30
Piercing The Bindu — 31
Integrating Awakening And Living The Truth — 34
Continuing Expansion After Awakening — 36
The Birth Of The Awakener Function — 37
Emptiness Fullness: The Experience Of Giving "Shaktipat" In The Awakened State — 38
Quantum Physics: A New Language Of Awakening — 41
Music, Sound, And Source — 44
The Synchronicity Paradigm: Balance Yields Wholeness — 48
Our Self-Destructive Human Game From The Viewpoint Of Enlightening Awareness — 50

Dr Richard Moss

- Introduction: Embodying Consciousness In Relationship — 55
- The Breakdown Of The Perceptual Matrix — 59
- Fundamental Realisation, The Absolute Perfection And Rightness Of All Things — 62
- The Birth Of aANew Sensitivity To Energy — 64
- Bringing Awakening Into Every Aspect Of Life — 67
- The Dark Night Of The Soul — 72
- The Second Fundamental Realisation: All Of Manifest Reality Is the Divine Mother — 79
- Awakening In Relationship Is An Endless Process — 82
- Vision – Inspiration – Expansion   84
- Man And Woman, The One That Has Become Two — 91
- Creativity And The Intelligence Of The Body — 98
- When The Earth Says No — 101

David Spero

- Introduction: Liberation through Kali's Fierce Grace — 109
- The Path — 112
- When the Mother Adopts Your Nervous System — 113
- Mother Reveals the Essence of the Four Yogas — 118
- You Can't Know It Because You Are It — 120
- Sahaja: Fully Embodying Consciousness 121
- Things Are As They Are — 123
- Floating In and Out of Bhavas — 124
- Speaking About the Earth — 127
- Spontaneous Functioning — 129
- Meditation Is Just Living Naturally — 131
- Everyone Is Presumed Innocent — 132
- No Splinter of Separation — 134
- Mother Takes Away All The States And Then All The States Are You — 136
- There's Something Functioning That Is Bigger Than Any of Us — 138
- Kali Took The In-dweller — 146
- Transmission: The Perfume Of The Mother — 149

Swami Shankaracharya

Introduction: The Eternal Unity Of Shiva And Shakti	155
Meetings With Great Yogis	158
God Alone Plays All The Roles: There Is Only That	160
Initiation Into Tantra – The Path Of The Mother	161
Within That Oneness You Can Still Improve Yourself On A Personal Level	163
Integration – Diversity Is Contained Within The Reality Of Unity	167
The Value Of Darshan	168
Consciousness Awakens To Itself – There Are No Enlightened People	171
It's The Shakti That's Giving Shaktipat	176
Seeing The Ego In The Context Of Reality	177
The Ego Of Knowledge And The Ego Of Doership	179
Conscious Embrace	183
The Earth Is An Inherent Identification In Consciousness	185
The Whole Universe Is Involved Right Here, Right Now	186
There Is Only THE Power; It's Not YOUR Power	189
The Practice Of Witness Awareness	192
Courting The Kundalini – We Owe Our Existence To That Great Power	194
The Sense Of "Who You Are" Is The Cloth Of The Mother	196
Identification Is The Problem – Not The Mind Itself	197
Everything Springs From The One	198

Conclusion: Classical Teachings On The Nature Of Kundalini

Kundalini: Her Three Aspects - By Swami Shankaracharya	202
Common Misconceptions - By Swami Shankaracharya	204

Glossary	207
Suggested Reading	226
Contact Information	229
About The Author	231

Foreward
By Kia Scherr

The Dance of Kundalini passionately beckons us into the arms of the Divine Feminine, also known as the Divine Mother, the fullest expression of life itself.

As we can see from these profound experiences of kundalini awakening, once we have accepted and become one with this embrace, life becomes a wild love affair, breaking our heart and mind wide open as identification with ego dissolves.

As I read these interviews one weekend in Mumbai, India in a hotel room that overlooks the Arabian Sea, my eyes kept moving from the words on the page to the endless flow of waves outside my window. Writing such as this which describes the most intimate of human experience, the experience of that which is beyond words, generating a ripple of energy deep inside my being that grows stronger as I continue to sit and read. I feel excited, grateful and humbled all at once as I gain a greater understanding of how this dance of life has played out in me over the years.

As you read these experiences for yourself, you will see that Kundalini, Divine Feminine, Divine Mother is not an esoteric concept reserved for the most ardent spiritual seeker. It is the vibrant life force that exists within the Soul of our Being, coiled in the root of our spine.

Once awakened, it stirs itself up in a unique way that disrupts the sleepy haze of non-awareness forever. Clouds that hung comfortably over our minds for years finally erupt, disengaging who we thought we were.

Reading this book will disrupt those clouds and re-arrange perceptions of what appeared to be reality as you knew it. If you open to the embrace awaiting you, you will allow this life force, the Divine itself to ignite a new awakening of consciousness that will alter your experience and transform you in the process. Correction: nothing is actually transformed – it just feels that way. It is our perception that is forever altered.

What we conceived of as 'enlightenment' is simply an experience of Oneness with life exploding all around us. When we experience this awakened energy within our individual consciousness it pulsates and moves in a sort of dance that destroys all previous notions of ourselves. We become fully present to it in the famous 'now' moment. That moment becomes our only moment, the only moment that ever is.

That's the joke, it is not a flash of lightening striking our big bad ego. It is a recognition of the endless moment that is so full it is bursting and that burst is the *energetic movement* of Consciousness that has been called 'kundalini' in the ancient traditions. This energy awakens us as it moves throughout our nervous system, taking on a life of its own within our 'little' life.

The ego doesn't matter anymore. It doesn't go away, no not at all. As you will see from these brilliant interviews, it is the opening of life into its own flow of existence that dominates the awareness, so that 'ego' is like an ant roaming around trying to sting an elephant but with no power in its bite.

This book is inviting us to dance, so here is an opportunity to accept a Divine invitation to partner with the Ultimate, which will be for each of us, a unique dance. If we surrender to this partner, we will swoon in ecstasy as it takes the lead around the dance floor of our lives.

Kia Scheer,
Co-founder of One Life Alliance

Kia Scheer
Co-founder of One Life Alliance

One Life Alliance is dedicated to raising the world's peace index through collaborations with businesses, governments and education.
One Life Alliance was founded in response to the Mumbai terrorist attacks of 2008 that took the lives of co-founder Kia Scherr's husband and 13 year old daughter. Our mission is to counter-balance terrorism with love and compassion as a way to increase the peace index in the world. We must honor the oneness and dignity of life in ourselves and in each other.

"Now is time for radical love. To live with boundless compassion, forgiveness and love in every interaction. Our survival as a human race depends on it" – Kia Scheer

Preface
A Celebration Of Possibility

The vision of this book is to explore, share, and celebrate the mystery of Kundalini Awakening. This is the awakening of the spiritual current within a human being, the dance of the Timeless with time. It's the dissolution/integration of the small sense of self into the Infinite Ocean of Being, and the subsequent full embodiment of that awakening in daily life. In this book I use the words, "Energetic Awakening." and "Kundalini Awakening interchangabilly

Principally, this is a book of intimate encounters with teachers who have undergone this process of Kundalini awakening in depth, and who teach with an emphasis on the awakening of the deeper energies in consciousness. Such *energetic awakening* is intrinsic to the process of incarnating or embodying the Larger Self in ordinary human life.

As the process of conducting the interviews for this book unfolded, a unique pattern emerged. During pivotal periods of their awakenings, each of the teachers had been graced with a profound encounter with the Divine Feminine. While the Divine Feminine, as such, is not the specific focus of this book, it does form an intrinsic part of the total weave, and is indeed a deep undercurrent theme in the spiritual journeys of each of the teachers featured herein.

Introduction
A Thing Should Be Compared, But Only Ever To Itself

Universal Life Energy is the very Source of our individual lives and minds, the substratum of the universe itself. Being our Source and substance, the nature of this energy, which is our own true nature, can be disclosed to us. When this disclosure/awakening "happens," the very structure of our being undergoes a radical transformation. The egoic viewpoint is uprooted as the self/other duality collapses, turning one's world upside down and inside out. Psychological time comes to an end, along with the illusion of self. Vast energies within the psyche are released and a new process of profound inner transformation begins to unfold. The functioning of this universal life energy in the process of spiritual unfoldment, and the resulting inner transformations in consciousness are the subject of this book.

I am not attempting to define what enlightenment is, nor even what energetic awakening is. I am, rather, embarking on a journey of celebration, delighting in this most remarkable process that is unfolding within the collective body of humanity – *the Embodiment of Consciousness, the Awakening of Spirit into Flesh*.

This book focuses on the process of ego dissolution and the resulting revelation of the Oneness of Being. It is not primarily concerned with the secondary energetic phenomena that may arise out of this deeper process. These phenomena may well be a part of the deeper process but they are not specifically the focus of this book.

I chose to share a little of my own story, simply to provide some background and a platform from which I explore and enquire with the various people you shall meet herein.

I will act as something of a guide as we journey together, partaking of the highs and lows, as well as the insights and wisdom that have arisen within each of these remarkable teachers by virtue of having undergone such profound inner transformations.

The interviews were approached in a relaxed manner, yet with a focus on penetrating into the heart of the process that had unfolded and was unfolding still within each person I interviewed. During the interviews I found the uniqueness of each teacher evoked remarkably different atmospheres and different lines of enquiry.

The settings for the interviews range from Master Charles' Still Point Monastery in the Blue Ridge Mountains of Virginia; a suburban organic farm, close to the home of Dr Richard Moss in Ojai, California; the happy metropolis of sunny Palm Springs and its utterly astounding Joshua Tree National Monument, with David Spero, and finally into the construction zone of a new ashram nestled in the hills of California's Topanga Canyon, with Swami Shankaracharya.

These interviews took me across America, on an energy- and insight-filled spiritual adventure. Along with an ever-growing appreciation for the uniqueness of all of our journeys, I was left with a deep sense of awe and wonder, and much gratitude for the generosity of everyone who shared so much and so openly on this wonderful journey.

Each of these remarkable human beings is a model of living with a deep awakening and our flawed humanity, side by side. My feeling is that teachers like these serve to remind us of what is within us, and inspire us to look there. While I have written a book about these remarkable human beings and have the greatest love and respect for them, I am in no way suggesting that you take their words as gospel. Rather, it is my hope that you will be left with a greater appreciation for the uniqueness of your own journey, and renewed courage to dive deeply within your own being, trusting in the unfathomable wisdom of the process that *is* unfolding within you.

My Own Journey with Kundalini

Many years ago, I found myself walking into a small upstairs room in a quiet suburb of Melbourne Australia to meet a man who, I had heard, had undergone a deep awakening into the unitive dimension of being. The man was Master Charles. (Then known as Brother Charles)

Through a series of seeming coincidences (I had been interested in sound technology and Kundalini awakening) I had been led to this room, and with great anticipation I awaited his entry. Up until this point in my spiritual journey I had been an ardent reader of teachers such as Jiddu Krishnamurti and Nisargadatta Maharaj, along with various Christian mystics such as St. Teresa of Avila and St. John of the Cross. More recently, I had been introduced to the late Nityananda of Ganeshpuri, and Baba Muktananda. Needless to say, I had high expectations.

When Master Charles entered the room, I observed him closely; he seemed to sway like a drunken elephant and moved very slowly. He was wearing what appeared to be a silk monk's garment (I would later learn that this was a gift to him from his guru, the late Baba Muktananda.) My mind was not at all impressed by any of this, for my image of an awakened sage was that he or she would be beyond image consciousness, simple and ordinary. Master Charles seemed to be full of a sense of theatre and show.

I sat disappointed, reviewing in my mind the great expense I had now accrued in getting to this disappointing meeting. *A fake,* I thought. I was in this state of total disillusionment, and free from expectation that anything might happen, when Master Charles started to casually gaze around the room (he still hadn't spoken). I was seated toward the back of the room, and when his gaze met mine, something happened that was outside of time and space. Suddenly a deep intuition arose within my heart that Consciousness is not separate. Like dry leaves caught in a swift strong wind, I could feel all prior conditioning based on separation crumble, and the tension that goes with it dissolve in a flash of timeless understanding. What happened next came totally out of the blue; I felt a subtle sensation within the region of my chest, almost as if a cork had been popped, then vast waves of Love began surging within my being. These waves just kept on coming, arising from somewhere deep within my own Self, and as they flowed, my whole being was saturated in Love. Suddenly it occurred to me that this Love was flooding the *whole universe*, filling and sustaining all and everything. At that recognition, my mind lost its hold, and I melted totally in the recognition that *there is enough love within each of us for all of us*. There is no shortage of Love. The universe is filled with it, and it is us.

I sat immersed in Love for the remainder of the program, literally swimming in a sea of Love and energy. I felt certain that I had come to meet this Divine Presence that animated all of Life and not a *separate* person. Though I understood and recognized that what Master Charles and all of us really are *IS* this animating Presence, and that this Presence was awake to itself through Master Charles.

A few days later, having been picked up from the airport by a friend, I found myself sitting silently in the back of the car on the long ride home. It was during this trip that a new process began to unfold, one that would change the inner landscape of my being forever. During the car ride, a spontaneous enquiry into the nature of "self" suddenly arose.

What happened was this: it occurred to me that "I" was the central hub of everything I did, yet I was ignorant of what this "I" actually was. I thought, how can I know if I even need enlightenment if I don't know the nature of the "I" that needs or wants?

Then quite suddenly and altogether spontaneously, my attention seemed to invert itself and focus on what appeared to be its centre, the "me-feeling." It was a feeling in my chest, an actual *physical sensation of contracted feeling*, and it was now being spontaneously focused on, without any sense of volition or choice. The question then arose deeply, and with great passion: "*What is this thing called me?*" My attention became riveted on this "me-sense," and thus a process of spontaneous self-enquiry began.

Paradoxically, I noticed that there was now more attention to give to the outside world. It was as if by shining the light of attention onto its Source, more light would arise from within, to light my way in the world. Effortlessly, this enquiry went on day after day, unhindered by any outward activity. With a penetrating inner glance, *attention focused itself* on this "feeling of me-ness." The question echoed relentlessly in my mind: "What is this thing called me?"

I felt deeply renewed, and realised that a quickening of my consciousness had taken place. I felt fundamentally changed. Yet this was to be only the prelude to something utterly beyond anything that can be known with the mind.

It was about six days into this enquiry when the process seemed to suddenly intensify greatly. I felt a deep urgency to find out the precise nature of this "me-sense." I decided to sit down on a comfortable couch and not get up until I had fully penetrated and understood the nature of "I." So I sat down on a small couch in my room, closed my eyes, and gave myself completely to the task of really penetrating into the nature of "self."

At this point I wasn't interested in anything called enlightenment; the farthest thing from my mind was wanting to attain any particular state. I wanted to know really "what I am," or, more precisely, what is at the root of the "I" feeling. What is this thing called "me?"

As I sat looking inward at the object of my contemplation, the "me-sense," attempting to penetrate to its core with one-pointed attention, sort of like using awareness as a sword, to cut through an apple to see what's at its core, I continued to become more and more deeply engrossed, and was perhaps many hours into this process (time which I did not notice passing,) when all of a sudden something momentous happened. *The sense of "me," the object of my contemplation, suddenly vanished.* Simultaneous with this event, my sense of having a body was also uprooted, and I had the sudden perception that my body had rushed into the distance, leaving "me" in a total void, except now there was no sense or feeling of "me-ness," no feeling of being localised, no body, no thing, no place.

"My mind," with its intent to enquire into the nature of "I," was still present enough to ask, " What do I do now? Into what do I enquire? There is only void! There is no me." Then, mysteriously, a female voice called from within, *Go into the Void. Dive into the Void.* Suddenly there was a sense that I, as "formless, conscious, nothingness," was shrinking down until I became smaller than the smallest, and alternating with this, "I" was expanding bigger than the biggest. These two bizarre sensations also appeared to exist within each other; I was infinitely big, and infinitely small. I knew there was nothing smaller than I, nor anything larger than I. However big a thing is, including the universe, I am bigger; however small a thing is, I am smaller. Concurrent with this was a sensation of hammering between my eyebrows, an intense pressure, as if at that point I was being hit with a sledgehammer. This all seemed to be happening simultaneously. It was not the sense of a body expanding; it was the sense of pure conscious nothingness expanding.

At that moment, quite unexpectedly and out of the Void of pure nothingness, there arose suddenly, and totally, *the direct revelation* of what IS, of what I AM. Vast, Silent, Total Being, the Absolute, pure Is-ness, not a thing, not involved at all with time and change, yet also the *very substance of all that passes*, unmoving, unbounded LIGHT. The Light that makes even darkness possible, it was of the nature of contentment.

I don't know how long there was a sitting still, but presently I opened my eyes and suddenly understood that "I" do nothing – I only AM. I make all things possible by virtue of being the only "reality" a thing could have. All things exist in my Light, and have their being in me, and I am no thing. As I stood up and walked to the wall of my room, I marvelled that there was *simply no separation* between I and the wall; I pervaded and was everything that was and wasn't. I felt a deep peace and knew directly that *nothing had ever happened,* as what I am is all there IS, and I have never undergone any change.

It dawned on me that this is what the sages speak of, this is self-knowledge. I walked outside and looked into space and there alone was I, spread out as infinite space. All the universe I saw has its being in me.

This new awareness was also a kind of joke, as I saw and knew I had always been this. It is the very Light that sees *anything*; even ignorance lives in this Light. I also understood that it was fundamentally no big deal what had happened, as nothing had really happened. I thought, *So what?* And found myself laughing, a few days later while grocery shopping. *It won't change the price of bread,* I mused.

Various insights arose as the days went on, although the only thing that had really changed, as far as I could see, was that now there was *no separation* between myself and the rest of the world, manifest or Unmanifest. Really what made the difference was the absence of the "me thought." Now, in the absence of the feeling of being a separate self centre, there was no "one" who was at the effect of anything that happened, and at the end of every action there was a certainty that *I had done nothing* – I simply was what I AM. I understood that thoughts "arise," there is no thinker. And likewise, actions "happen", it was seen that the body just moved *of itself*. All action, I saw, was a kriya, or spontaneous action.

As well, I had the deep intuition that this was now another process beginning. Rather than a final awakening, I saw this as an opening, an opening into a deeper dimension of consciousness, an opening which I intuited would continue to deepen and unfold. Also I saw that everything just happened, but I didn't at all know what was causing things to happen. There was within me a deep feeling that the next phase of this understanding was the revelation of the power or dynamism of the Self, what I could intuit as a *feminine energy*, that was at the very heart of phenomenal manifestation and miraculously doing all doings. I had been blessed with an opening to the eternal stillness, the Unmanifest, but was yet to know the fullness of the Divine Energy, the Mother of the ten thousand things.

I did, however, feel this power in my being as a *subtle current of life energy* that arose out of my Unmanifest nature as light, into the phenomenal realm and localized itself in the region of my brow. It was felt as an intense throbbing physically, and as a sweet current of Presence at a subtle level. While I saw all this occurring within my physical and subtle self, I also intuitively paid it no special attention, as what *I AM was the seeing through of all phenomena including this*. Yet a strange intuition also told me that this subtle current of life energy was the first caress of the Mother, the feminine power that is at the heart of all nature and manifest life.

A new interior process had begun, one that would take me years to understand and cooperate fully with, a process that is still unfolding and that I am still learning. I now see that, even though we may be blessed with an understanding of our eternal nature, on the level of our physical life in our bodies, minds, and hearts, there may still be a mountain of conditioning – maybe ancient conditioning – that is rooted in *the fundamental illusion of being separate*. At this early stage in the process, I would intuitively ignore all thoughts and movements of mind that arose out of this ignorance. This, I feel, is what dissolves them in light, restoring gradually our body and mind into a position of subservient harmony with our eternal nature. It has taken me many, many years of living with this amazing process to even begin to learn to ride the process in the direction it wants to take, and to let go into it, in *faith*.

Over the years this has been an ongoing process, and is more of an "unfolding of what is from within," as opposed to a process in linear time.

In the midst of all this intense inner unfolding, the unfolding of a whole new dimension of consciousness, I lived a relatively normal life – working, travelling, in relationships, and continuing to explore the many spiritual traditions of the world. On one occasion I went to my local church prayer group, as I had what seemed to be an insatiable appetite for devotional activities, which for me were always an honouring of the Living Presence that was pulsating within my own heart. I happened to be friends with a few of the local Catholic priests and on this occasion, a small group of people had gathered to sing in praise of the Holy Spirit. As the prayer and singing unfolded, I suddenly found myself filled with intense inner vibrations and felt intensely drawn to a large painting of Jesus that was hanging on the wall. As I gazed at the painting, the flow of energy within me expanded, and accelerated into the cyclonic force that up until then had only unfolded with such intensity in the presence of Master Charles. Now it was exploding and dancing within me in the midst of a church youth group. Spontaneous humming took hold of my being and suddenly I felt myself intuitively let go into the sweetest love. Simultaneously, an immense peace descended. I felt the entire room and beyond was saturated in a shower of liquid peace, which seemed to drench the very pores of my skin, flood my heart and utterly still my mind.

After this event I walked aimlessly through the streets, flooded with peace, walking in a rain of grace. I felt that I had been utterly cleansed, inside and out, with a peace that was so sweet and so delicate.

I must add a crucial detail at this point. Many years after the initial event, a friend and I were singing and dancing in the street, calling out playfully to passers-by that all is illusion, it's all a dream. After this we went to a nearby park to relax, and as my friend was speaking to me, suddenly the "me-sense" re-arose. Now, there was once again an "I" who appeared to be listening, whereas a few moments prior there was only listening. My first thought was, *Oh shit. Suffering's back!* Then suddenly it was *seen* that this too is just another phenomenon arising. The me-sense itself was seen to be an object, like any other object that appears in consciousness.

It was almost impossible to express what was happening within me to friends and family, and so for the most part, I chose to remain silent.

On one level, there has been great upheaval, as the deeper energies awakened effect profound psychological and emotional purification, often causing deep-seated psychic knots and areas of unconscious conditioning to surface into the body-mind. When this happens it's a deeply impactful, experiential happening. There have been and continue to be periods of great inner unrest and emotional pain, as childhood hurts surfaced to be relived and purified in the living presence of noumenal energy. In a way, living with this process appears to intensify the awareness of one's limitations and suffering, as the body-mind now has a tremendously heightened sensitivity, due to the increased flow of energy within it.

Yet, I must clarify here that I am not speaking of an energy that merely flows "within the physical form" or even within the various subtle bodies. All bodies, subtle or physical, themselves "exist within this field of silence and timeless Presence." It is the very space within which the planets rotate. This Space, or Beingness itself, is unfolding and moving as energy *within itself*, an energy that is utterly transcendent of the body-mind, within which the body-mind arises and has its being. This transcendent energy simultaneously floods and animates this body and all of manifest life. This transcendent Presence IS what is living through all of us.

Overall, there has been a gradual shift in my orientation to the world, into seeing and relating to the "World *as* Self." Even though the original "in-seeing" utterly confirmed this fact of World as Self, what was known in the core of Being had to ripple through the body-mind's conditioning, melting away layers of concepts rooted in the illusion of separation. As one layer is cleared, a new layer may surface. And each layer of old conditioning that surfaces carries its own karmic relationship to the world. By this I mean to underscore the fact that mind and world are not separate. So when a particular pattern of mind is functioning, the world literally mirrors that pattern of mind. Thus, awakening or energetic opening can render one's inner *and* outer worlds more luminous, fluid, dynamic, *and,* simultaneously, more transparent to pain, suffering and darkness.

I have found that simplicity is a key, just stepping out of the mind's spin, allowing it to be, but *not to define who we are*. Always resting more and more in the unknown, the uncreated, the unbounded Presence, from which I learn, again and again, all real intelligence and grace flow, which is the source of all healing, and all blessing.

Prelude To The Interviews: Mystical Vision Of A Sage

The night before I was to depart for the USA, I lay on the floor of my girlfriend's bedroom, feeling the demands of final preparations building in my body as a mass of tension. As I tried to drift off to sleep, I started to feel the familiar pressure of the "prana" increasing in the crown of my head. My gut-level response was "Oh no. Not now. I need to get some sleep." I tossed and turned, wishing the energy would let me rest. I knew well that such nights of increased energetic flow most often meant that, instead of the usual sleep, I would spend the night drifting in deeply expanded states, with an electric heat pouring through my body, the pressure and intensity of which is often almost too much to bear. As I lay on the floor, the tension of resisting this energetic process was mounting. Then, quite unexpectedly, I saw directly into my mind's resistance to this phenomenon, *which is the very essence of our mind's constant activity*: avoiding what is painful and deemed not useful in its ego-based world, and chasing after future-based pleasures and desires. With this insight, my mind suddenly released its grip and, in place of the mental tension that had been present, a deep current of peace filled my entire being; simultaneously, awareness expanded dramatically, and subject-object consciousness melted away. The entire universe suddenly fell away below me, as I found myself hurtling upward, dilating in circumference and rapidly expanding into an oceanic Oneness. My mind was filled with the echoing words "beyond space-time," as if these words were a statement of intent to pierce the veil of manifest existence. Stars and clusters of light rushed by with tremendous speed, in a visionary encounter with the universe that was utterly awe-inspiring. Now aware of myself as an ocean of space, a literal sea of universal silence and stillness, I saw the whole cosmos vibrating within my own unlimited being as a mere pattern of energy, electric and mandala-like in nature, a ripple of movement within an oceanic sea of Oneness and Silence. Suddenly a voice arose from within the vast space of oceanic consciousness: "You are space-time itself." All at once a vision filled my awareness and I found myself sitting in a cave at the feet of the great sage Sri Ramana Maharshi. Ramana was young and filled with all the vigour of youth.

I sat in a state of total wonderment, gazing at the sage; the only thought arising in my mind was *This is my own self*. As I gazed at the young Ramana, he suddenly started singing to me in the most beautiful melodic voice, directing his gaze slightly over my shoulder, as if singing to an audience that was behind me that I could not see. He sang something to the effect of "Yes, yes, this is a very good enquiry; dive deep into the radiance of the Self. The radiance of being has its source in the Self. That radiance manifests as the life force in all beings. Trace it back to its Source." His voice was full of sheer delight, as I simply sat and listened in awe. Suddenly the vision ended and I found myself back on the floor of my girlfriend's room, now filled with an ambrosial peace, deep joy and renewed enthusiasm for the project at hand, as well as feeling that I had been deeply blessed. As I lay there, my mind empty yet filled with peace, a poem suddenly sprang into my mind:

> Stop chasing desires and running from fears
> Rest in the center
> Elixir of Radiance

Thus began my trip to the United States to interview four remarkable human beings. I am utterly delighted to share this adventure with you through the pages of this book.

Master Charles Cannon

Introduction
Iconoclastic Modern Mystic

A Tantric Master of the highest order and an iconoclastic modern mystic, Master Charles Cannon took the vows of monkhood known as Sannyas in India, thus joining the ancient Vedic/Tantric tradition, the world's oldest religious order. During his initiation he was given the name Swami Vivekananda by his own master, Baba Muktananda. After returning to the West following his twelve years in India, Swami Vivekananda took on the name Brother Charles, which he felt was more appropriate in the Western context. This later evolved into Master Charles at the request of his students. The term Swami literally means "Master of oneself."

Master Charles radiates an immense and palpable field of transformational energy, and in this interview that was certainly the case. As I engaged in conversation with Master Charles, I found myself flooded with the most sacred of *vibrational fields*, as if in his presence the whole universe opened up, revealing its innermost secrets. In the guru's world, this transmission is a natural and spontaneous happening; it is simply Love communicating itself, to itself, for the sake of itself. This process, known as Shaktipat (literally, energy-transfer), often effects great changes and spontaneous awakenings in many of those who are drawn to visit him and other great gurus.

Having undergone a deep spiritual awakening in his early childhood, the young Charles lived a relatively normal life outwardly, while inwardly his world was the domain of the Mother. His was a world in which the profound transformational energies of consciousness worked their magic, effecting great changes in the innermost recesses of his being. During these early years, young Charles was blessed with ongoing visionary experiences of the Divine Mother, visions he refers to as *the apparition*. These encounters with the "apparition" gently and consistently expanded his awareness, eventually flowering into the fullness of Divine Awakening in his adult years, under the guidance and tutelage of his own Master.

Master Charles may be said to be the living embodiment of the Tantric ideal of Conscious Embrace, celebrating and affirming all of life as an *equal expression* of the One. Wholeheartedly embracing our modern world, he specifically utilizes advances in sound technology in the service of conscious evolution. He recognizes that our inherent Divine nature Shines, no matter what the times or cultures we find ourselves in. "Everything," he affirms again and again, "is a celebration of consciousness." He is a Divine Jester and Crazy Wisdom Master, forever pointing out the absurdity of our human masks, and then suggesting (as we laugh) that our very laughter is the Divinity we are looking for, right under our noses.

While he has already written a detailed account of his own energetic awakening in his book *The Bliss of Freedom*, I felt that this interview would allow me to explore the territory afresh.

In order to give us a platform from which to launch, I undertook the interviews with some basic themes in mind. The topics I hoped to cover were Master Charles' early childhood experiences, which included profound and transformational mystical visions of the Divine Mother, his subsequent full Kundalini awakening during his twelve years of living with his own Master, and finally the piercing of the Blue Pearl, resulting in the full and spontaneous abidance in and *as* Non-dual Consciousness. However, I soon learned that interviews of this nature have a life of their own.

After a gruelling flight from Australia, which included a twelve-hour layover at Los Angeles Airport, I finally arrived at Master Charles' home, which he calls The Still Point Monastery, a modern-day spiritual sanctuary nestled high in the Blue Ridge Mountains of Virginia. Utterly exhausted and sleep-deprived, I had few days in which I could rest, and then along with extensive interviews with Master Charles, I was to be participating in a week-long retreat called the Mastery Program, with people who had gathered from all over the world.

I wasn't at all prepared for the jet lag, and my readjustment to the American time zone wasn't easy, yet as the days passed I found myself progressively relaxing. As my mind began to quieten, I found myself in the most magical of environments, high in the Blue Ridge Mountains, where Master Charles has been living for many years with a small community of truth lovers.

All around us squirrel and deer played about in the autumn leaves, as, from speakers in the trees and on the rooftops, ancient mantras sounded against a background of beautiful celestial music. Specially designed rooms, set aside for massage and various types of *energetic balancing* sessions, dotted the landscape. I marvelled at the beautiful meditation hall that had been designed according to the ancient principles of sacred geometry and hand-built by the monastic residents. Everything in the environment was clearly intended to support the inner awakening process by fostering balance and evoking a sense of the sacred. Indeed, it was akin to a heavenly realm, hidden away in the Virginia mountains.

Spontaneous Childhood Awakening

Could you speak to me about your early spontaneous spiritual awakenings? What exactly was the nature of those experiences? And when did they first begin?

The earliest recollection of spiritual experience was at about the age of three. I would have apparitions during the night in my bedroom. I would wake from sleep and see a figure standing at the end of my bed, who was not a normal human being, but much more luminous and ethereal. It didn't frighten me because the energy that accompanied it was very expansive, elevating, nurturing, motherly, very blissful. There was nothing fearful about it.

That experience continued all through my early childhood until the form of the apparition became clear. It was the Virgin Mother of Catholicism. Since I was raised a Catholic, that data was everywhere surrounding me and that is the manifestation of God, or Source, that I thus initially experienced in my early childhood.

As a small child, the apparition was confined to my sleep time, my alone time. As I aged into the more formative years, both the apparition and the state of being that accompanied it, the expanded elevated state of wholeness, or unified Consciousness, the euphoria, the bliss, the perception of the play of Consciousness, of reality as a living vibrating consciousness, unfolded outside of my sleep time, spontaneously here, there and everywhere.

This brings to my mind an interesting point: that most people don't have a consistent experience of a higher energy as a factor in their life, and with enculturation, the sense of ego as separate from life can become quite compounded. Therefore, when they have an awakening to a higher energy, there can be a great deal of friction between the old and the new, which can be experienced as, "Oh, I'm dying; I'm losing my sense of self into something larger that's absorbing me," but it seems that your journey was very smooth.

Yes, very smooth. There was no fear because the apparition was so nurturing. Everything that was conveyed to me when she spoke was always in terms of me being her child and great love, bliss and light, just elevated to states of euphoria. It felt so good and I associated it with that experience so there was no question of fear. There was nothing at all to fear.

Were there marked developments in the flow or depth of mystical awareness, or in the depth of awakening that happened at an early stage before you met Muktananda?

It was very consistent. Yet, it progressively and spontaneously increased. Here, there, in the midst of whatever was happening, I would spontaneously elevate to the state of unified consciousness, or I would see the apparition. The frequency and the consistency increased, all through my formative years, teenage years into my early twenties when I met Muktananda.

I was informed via the apparition that whatever happened was a preparation and that even though I might not understand it, I should just experience it, and that one day I would understand, one day all of my experience would make sense. It would be like a kaleidoscope that would all fall into place. All that was essential at that point in my life was to simply experience the experience and trust that it was part of a process, a plan, a destiny, that I would fully understand when the time was right. It was this divine communion that put me at ease. So I had that kind of support, that trust, that communication, that just relaxed me.

I also had many questions that inspired my interest in studying related topics. I became very interested at an early age in things mystical, religious, spiritual, metaphysical, etc., but that inquiry was born out of my experience. I wanted to know, well, if I were the only one who ever had this experience. Through the study of comparative religion and philosophy, mysticism and metaphysics I learned, of course, that I was not and that this was an authentic process. I was able to fully trust in it, to flow with it and watch it unfold.

Are you saying that because the apparition was informing you and guiding you, that there was not any cultural conflict?

In general, no. Not really. I was raised in a normal American middle-class Catholic family. Religion and church were a regular part of life. I went to Catholic school and was supported in religious experience from an early age. The enculturation of the surrounding world did not differ that much from my familial experience.

There was minimal conflict until I became a teenager which is, of course, when everybody enters into a more conflicted experience. Yet, whenever I had conflict, I simply asked the apparition, and it was always resolved. No matter what, the question always was: how did this spiritual experience, this mystical experience that was a major part of my life from my earliest years, fit into everything I was now experiencing? I was always told that there was no conflict. I was simply to experience everything that unfolded and that there was nothing wrong with any of it.

It was all about experience. I was given a great freedom to explore, to experience everything that presented itself as appropriate and as part of this learning process that I would one day understand. So I did exactly that and as a result I didn't have much conflict. I had guidance that I trusted. It answered all my questions and I just kept rolling along.

Visions Of God As Mother – The Apparition

The experience of the apparition, could you tell me more about the nature of that occurrence? You said there was an energetic presence and vibration that you felt within. As well as experiencing the apparition to be an objective phenomenon, was the apparition completely conscious? Even more conscious than a normal human being, perhaps?

Absolutely, yes.

You could interact...

Absolutely.

Eyes open, speaking...

Yes, just like another human being standing there, albeit translucent so that you could clearly distinguish that it wasn't as dense as another human being. All the subtle dimensional luminosity and the ethereal qualities of mystical apparition were actualized.

Usually the energetic vibration came first; I would sense the energy, the vibration that was expansive and similar to what I experienced in church. As a young child you go into a church and it's quiet and peaceful, and you sense that energetic vibration. What I experienced was like the church coming to me.

Then it would increase into a saturating peace and with it would come fragrances. Always the fragrances of roses and gardenias. And then the celestial sounds, like the tinkling of glass wind chimes and a very ethereal-sounding music. Again, just slowly saturating the environment. Then it would coalesce into the apparition and she would appear.

So, your sense of it was that the peaceful energy "itself" formed into the Mother?

Yes. She emerged from within it. The energy came first, then the form, and then the form would leave and the energy would slowly dissipate. It continues in this way even today. It has never stopped. As a child, I was more separate from it. Progressively, I've become more merged with it. It is always available, always guiding, always that very palpable divine presence and guidance.

Meeting The Master – Radical Expansion

So now we've gone through your childhood experiences of the Divine Mother, which became more consistent, appearing in more and more normal circumstances. Then you met Muktananda. I'm wondering, how radically did your contact with Muktananda's energy open up your own deepest-felt sense of yourself and life?

Well, quite radically, because Muktananda was the ultimate teacher; he was the living, eating, breathing, human embodiment of holistic, enlightening, liberated human experience. I had been well prepared. The Divine Mother had told me that the teacher was coming. That's what I had been prepared for, I didn't know precisely in what form, but I knew the teacher was coming, the one who would answer all my questions and bring that kaleidoscope together.

It wasn't a surprise, but it was very impactful. It had to be impactful enough that I would drop everything and pursue it, which is exactly what I did. I had to go to the other side of the world to meet him. I took a while to get there, but at quiet places along the way – a church, a holy man's shrine, a mosque – always the guidance came. It was usually her voice or the voice of the saint whose shrine I was visiting giving the same message: "Go to Muktananda; Muktananda will show you the way." So, when I met

Muktananda in person, there was no doubt whatsoever that it was where I belonged and would remain.

Shortly after meeting him in person, I had a meditative visionary experience in which I was sitting in a room at a big table, like a conference table. There was a door opposite and through the door came Muktananda, followed by the Divine Mother. She was carrying a scroll. They unrolled it on the table and it was the blueprint of my life. She then instructed him on what I needed to be taught and what had to be done. We all agreed that this is what would happen and then it unfolded. Thus the path was always very clear to me.

He was the model and I had to spend time with him to learn how to embody wholeness, how to be Source as a human being, and that I would have a similar destiny to his, which of course he always confirmed. It was very impactful and still is. I continue to see him. It's not that such Masters die and are gone. Death is just changing clothes and it's not a big deal in terms of the subtler dimensions of Consciousness, where forms of Consciousness continue their evolution. If you make yourself subtle, you can commune with them. Thus I have continuing connection and guidance.

Muktananda was a radically enlightened human being and the state of Consciousness that he modeled was the ultimate. I had the ultimate model and I was thoroughly trained under his thumb and at the same time entrained by his wholeness that just meditated me.

What was the progression in your inner world? In other words, given that you were already so incredibly sensitive and already had an awareness of energy, how did Muktananda's presence and Shakti influence your own state of being?

The word is amplitude. Muktananda amplified the power to the most palpable level possible. It was a palpable, Sourceful, Divine, saturating presence, 24 hours a day. So amplitude is the word with Muktananda. It made the experience constant and consistent. There were peaks and valleys within it, yet always a palpable and comprehensive wholeness that was amplified more and more, day-by-day. It was like you were living in heaven.

Many times I would think I needed to pinch myself: was this real? It was like being time-warped, suspended in a heavenly, euphoric, divine experience. Everything was dripping with grace and bliss. Vibrating consciousness, bliss, pleasure, and euphoric states. There's nothing else that has any importance, yet periodically you say "Wow, is this real?" You know? But of course, every time I pinched myself, it was real.

The Only Suffering I Ever Had Was When I Tried to Figure It Out

So many people suffer, they want this awakening, and they read about someone like Muktananda and it might as well be a story about another time on another planet, because it's so far removed from most people's experience. It seems like you've never had that big contrast between years of suffering, separation, anxiety, and fear, followed by a mystical awakening. You had years of mystical experience, followed by a massive expansion of what was already unfolding within you.

Yes, you are correct. My mystical experience unfolded in my early childhood and then naturally and progressively increased. It started very early on. The only suffering I ever had was when I tried to figure it out. When I was confused and couldn't understand, the only answer received was: "Just experience and one day it will all make sense. Through experience it will all be made clear." I learned to trust, based on the experience.

You're correct that there was no real struggle or Dark Night of the Soul. People often ask me: "What about the Dark Night of the Soul?" I respond by saying that if you are supposed to experience it you will. It simply was not part of my experience. I understand it within the context of mystical experience. Some people have it and some don't. My experience very naturally and progressively unfolded and it is still unfolding. I think that's the beautiful message of the living model of the master that I had with Muktananda,

The important point, that Muktananda so brilliantly modeled, is that the state of enlightenment is not static or stagnant. You don't reach an endpoint after which nothing else happens. Rather, it is progressive, ever increasing, subtler and subtler. I observed that evolutionary enlightenment in Muktananda and I also observe it in myself.

Therefore, in that understanding I say to myself and to everyone, there will always be more: God, Source, Consciousness, is an eternal forever. There will always be more. Muktananda perfectly modeled the enlightening experience. It was important because if you don't have the living embodiment, how are you going to know it?

The beauty of it was that in Muktananda, I had the best model I could possibly have had. I was able to experience the evolutionary unfoldment of unified Consciousness in a human being just like myself. Now, I can progressively observe and watch that same experience in myself.

The Path Of Guru Yoga

Could you perhaps speak about the concept of the guru as the way, the path of Guru Yoga as you experienced it?

There is an Eastern philosophical principle that delineates the most evolved path as that of constant association with the enlightened Master. The analogy given is that if you want to experience a suntan, you place yourself in the proximity of the sun 24/7 and then the suntan is inevitable. Muktananda placed great emphasis on this principle, and often quoted from Kashmir Shavism, which is the update of the philosophy of holism called the Tantra. He quoted from one of its core works the Shiva Sutras.

One of the main sutras is "Gururupayah" which in Sanskrit means "The Guru is the means." Without the Master, you have nothing, because in these philosophies of holism, the Master embodies the principle of grace, the empowerment that awakens the disciple and initiates the evolutionary unfolding of progressive wholeness and enlightening experience. That being said, my experience with Muktananda was an experience whose time had come.

As I wrote in detail in my autobiography, my experience came first from a photograph through which I received his grace, his empowerment. It was so truthfully impactful that nothing I had experienced in the whole of my life to that moment could compare to the depth of that experience. So therefore I wanted to know about it. To find him, I therefore went to the other side of the world, to India, to meet him. When I finally arrived at his ashram, he said, "Ah, ha! You've come! I've been waiting for you! This is your home, this is where you belong." We had a close relationship from Day One. I remained with him for twelve years, the last twelve years of his life. I became his closest Western disciple, which was quite extraordinary given that we didn't have a common language or culture. Again, it was the experience whose time had come.

Nothing is more powerful than the experience whose time has come. Our close association was exactly as delineated in the philosophical tradition. If you want to get a suntan, place yourself in the proximity of the sun. That much I understood: when I was in his presence, I experienced incredible empowerment and evolution in my own Consciousness. Therefore, it made great sense to me to simply glue myself to his feet and that's what I did. I stayed consistently with him through those twelve years.

It is also said in that tradition, that initially the guru and the disciple are two, from the disciple's perspective, but, progressively, if it is authentic, the two must become one. This was my experience over the years of our association: that all that was dualistic became non-dualistic, and what was fragmented became whole and unified in Consciousness. That was and still is our relationship.

Going Beyond The Distinction Of I And Thou

That brings up the somewhat philosophical, existential consideration of the subject/object distinction. Can you speak about your own experience of total identification with consciousness and going beyond the distinction of I and thou?

What you are addressing is the progression in relative reality from fragmentation or separation to wholeness and unification. All and everything evolves through relative experience, because human experience is governed by relative reality. We exist and experience within the relative arena. Within the more involved and the less evolved stages of manifestation, there is imbalance in the relative polarities that causes the illusion of separation. Yet, the journey of evolving Consciousness is to balance the relative polarities and to merge them.

Through balance comes wholeness, so progressively there has to be the experience of separation – the illusion that you and the object of your perception are separate and different. You and the other person, you and the tree, you and the universe around you are somehow more than one. Ultimately, it culminates in the merging of all relative polarities, so that you and all and everything, the "I" and "it," become the same Consciousness.

It is a progressive process of ever-increasing integrative wholeness as Consciousness evolves its primary intention to fully be itself. My experience is not different in that regard, in that your balance progressively becomes more and more precise, and your perception shifts based on the expansion of your awareness. As your awareness expands, you are more unified or more holistic in that awareness. That is what changes your perception. You then perceive that all and everything is really the same Consciousness.

This happens as you are progressing from a denser level to a more subtle level of manifestation. At the densest level, physical, mental, and emotional, everything appears quite solid around you. The walls, the furniture, the natural environment, other people, rooms, nature, everything appears solid. It is therefore easy to get caught in the illusion that it's all really separate and different. Yet, as Consciousness evolves its wholeness and moves from dense to subtle, things are no longer solid. What you assumed was a solid wall is now a vibrating dance of energy. What you assumed was the solid natural environment around you is now shimmering and glistening, disappearing and reappearing.

Based on the actualization of the subtler dimensions of your Consciousness, your perception is more holistic and unified. And when that is happening, your whole experience, your whole perception, is that it's all made out of the same stuff. Your experience and perception is that it's all one. There is only one. Everything is vibrating – everything. Whether I look at me or you, or anything, it all has the same vibratory dance of one Consciousness. There simply isn't anything solid or separate. There's more empty space than there is solidity in the whole of reality.

So, separation and duality is the great illusion that the truth dissolves. I often say that truth disempowers illusion. As you evolve to a truthful state of experience, the illusion shifts, the matrix dissolves. The matrix in terms of separation and duality dissolves into the oceanic oneness of Consciousness. Whether you term it Source, God, Consciousness or love, you are describing the same truthful reality.

Love is the positive polarity the opposite of which is fear. Fear is the expression of an imbalanced relative experience. It is a dense-dimensionally dominant experience mired by the illusion of separation. There are illusory "others" that you fear. If everything is one at the unified level of experience, what is there to fear? If there is no other, fear merges into love, or you could say love disempowers fear. So, it's the same no matter how you term it. You are truthfully essentially describing the holistic nature of reality. Whether you term it Source, God, Consciousness or love, all denote the same.

I have once again become present to the fact that you are a unique example of an enlightening consciousness inasmuch as you didn't have that background of seeking, separation, and fear. There was always within you a sense of energy and Oneness that simply increased and increased.

Yes, you are correct however, we all have to experience what we are not, so that relationally we can experience what we are.

Through all the formative years of my enculturation, I experienced exactly that... illusion, separation and fragmentation. I just didn't get identified and stuck. Most people get stuck in identification. I was able to quickly move through it. By the time I was twenty years old I was on my way to a consistent holistic experience with a Master.

Yet, it's not to say that I didn't have any of that experience at all. I did have that experience and can certainly relate to the seeker who must move through that illusory identification and its progressive disentanglement.

The Play Of Energy Manifests Through Our Concepts

The insight that the play of energy manifests through our concepts is a big part of your teaching and experience. Can you speak about where that specific understanding arose in your own journey?

Such understanding comes with any study of comparative religion and philosophy, which was my formative educational focus. I wanted to understand my own mystical experience and that led me into comparative religion and philosophy before I met my teacher.

If you study Zen or any of the great wisdom traditions, there's quite a detailed delineation of how the mind works. Under Muktananda's tutorial guidance, of course, I was very thoroughly trained in Tantric philosophy, which details the mechanics of Consciousness as it evolves itself in human experience, and how multi-dimensional data or information flavors our experience. I had the holistic education and simultaneously was living the holistic lifestyle wherein I was able to experience my concept. With an enlightened teacher, I could get guidance and clarification day in and day out and observe his interactions with thousands of people from all the different cultures of the world.

I observed that the basic human being is the basic human being. We are all living databases; we're all programmed computers, so to speak. We have our software package from our particular enculturation, and for the most part we're expressing it like any computer when you turn it on and play its software. A human being expresses the software of its enculturation, its conditioning.

Yet, once you awaken to that truth, you also awaken to the understanding that the data evolves. It's not static and fixed. You are not programmed and limited with your software for the rest of your days; Consciousness evolves through human experience and is constantly changing its data, so your database is being updated with every breath you take. Therefore, your data changes and likewise, you can change your data.

From the disciple's perspective, it's empowering to learn that you can change your data and therefore your experience. Once you are aware and know how your data affects you, then you're at choice, and you can change it. You can reprogram your computer, and that becomes a very important process in the experience of any disciple. It's an empowerment that says, "Okay, I begin with a truthful self-diagnostic; this is where I am, this is my database. Yet, my intention is to create a certain experience, and that experience is called wholeness. There are definite things I can do to change and transform my experience. This process has to do with my mind, my database and my software."

Piercing The Bindu

I'd like to know and hear about the piercing of the Blue Pearl, that is, entering the "Bindu."

Yes.

As I understand it, beyond the Bindu is the realm beyond the mind, where the mind just cannot follow. This is where I guess I am asking you to speak about the unspeakable, perhaps?

First of all, you have to understand that what is called the Blue Pearl, which in Sanskrit is Neela Bindu, means the "Blue Point," and is a symbol. It is a symbol within a particular culture and its holistic cosmology. It is meant to symbolize your soul, or what I term the Sourcepoint of your individuated Consciousness.

The Sourcepoint is the power source of the multidimensional human form that surrounds it. From the subtlest to the densest levels, through seven dimensions which correspond to the seven chakras, or the seven vortices. The Sourcepoint is the origination point of your individuated Consciousness and in the centre of them is the essence, the power source, your particular consciousness that is simultaneously one with the whole of universal Consciousness.

It is important to understand that not everyone has to experience the Blue Pearl symbolism. If it's not part of your software, you wouldn't experience it. It was my teacher's enculturated software, it therefore became a part of my experience as his disciple and I also experienced that same symbolism. But, everyone does not have to experience the Blue Pearl. Everyone experiences according to their own data and their own symbolism. There are many different traditions of mystical experience. Each symbolizes the Sourcepoint in a different way.

The experience of proximity to the Sourcepoint is very subtle dimensional reality in the centre of the crown vortex, or the supra-causal dimension of your multidimensional being. The evolutionary progression is from form into formlessness, from the fullness of manifestation into the emptiness of non-manifestation.

The Sourcepoint is very subtle holistic experience. Yet, what does it really symbolize? The perfect delineation would be the Taoist symbol, the yin-yang symbol. It symbolizes the perfect balance of relative polarities. When there is perfect relative balance, Consciousness tracks its origin, its Sourcepoint. It shifts its emphasis from Becoming into Being, from fullness to emptiness and its origin is in the positive polarity, or in being.

The explosion of the Sourcepoint symbolizes the unification of individuated Consciousness. It is the supra-causal level of pure Being and the high amplitude of holistic power permeates all the dimensions from subtle to dense. The resultant experience is unified Consciousness or wholeness. It is what some traditions term enlightenment.

That's the symbolism in which you experience the Sourcepoint and thereafter remain constant in its actualization. It is often described as emptiness, but a luminous emptiness, not an opaque emptiness or nothingness. What does that mean? It means emptiness with awareness or absence with some presence. How is that possible? Within relative reality, you cannot have one polarity without the other. One polarity can dominate the other, but not eliminate it. Therefore, in the extreme dominance of emptiness, there must be some fullness. It is the awareness within formless, empty Being. That is the experience of the Sourcepoint.

The explosion of the Sourcepoint is the merging of the relative polarities into one undifferentiated whole or one Source Consciousness. Thereafter, there is constant or substantiated wholeness. The illusion of separation is forever obliterated.

But again, the Blue Pearl is just a particular symbol that not everyone experiences. It symbolizes the unified level of relative reality. Beyond relative reality is the Void, which is beyond all experience since all experience is relative. The relative is absorbed back into the Void when the Creation Game ends.

Finished...

Until the Creation Game ends, we are all individuated Consciousness at some evolutionary level of relative reality. We can evolve to the subtlest level, the Blue Pearl, the Sourcepoint, and progress to subtler and subtler levels of wholeness, dwell there, and remain subtler and subtler and subtler and more and more comprehensive in our wholeness, but we can't leave the game. It's not possible until we, within the game, end the game.

The whole game goes...

Until the game goes, we are still in the game.

We're part of the game.

That's right, part of the play.

We're a chess piece itself.

That's right, exactly.

Beautiful.

Integrating Awakening and Living the Truth

Okay, living truth. How did you integrate that experience, that awakening, into your body and your mind, your relationships, and your daily life? And what, if any, challenges did you face in that integration process?

You don't have any choice. Once you experience a consistent unified consciousness, its power and amplitude permeates and saturates all and everything. There's nothing to do because doing is illusion that has been eliminated. It is experiential, not conceptual.

The emphasis is on experience and this is where many get confused and create what I call conceptual enlightenment, or intellectual enlightenment. They read a lot of books and their intellectual knowledge becomes a substitute for the actual experience. Yet, in truth, it's a vibrational, energetic experience and it is impossible to understand without the experience.

When you begin the journey, you are an involved, individuated Consciousness. Your dominant dimensionality is the physical, emotional, and mental. As your Consciousness evolves, it progresses from the dominance of the physical, emotional, and mental to the subtle, causal, and supra-causal. Each of these dimensions has a frequency of vibration based on the oscillation of the relative polarities therein. As you progress, your frequency of vibration changes.

At the densest level, you have a very slow vibrational frequency, and slow vibrational frequencies have low amplitude, and minimal power. The majority of humanity, mired in the physical, emotional, and mental dimensions of experience, has minimal power and amplitude. They believe they have the most power because that's where illusion and separation are dominant.

As Consciousness becomes more unified in the subtle dimensions, it relinquishes illusion and the frequency of vibration accelerates. The frequency of vibration in the subtle dimensions is at the speed of light and beyond toward infinite velocity. Linear reality dissolves into simultaneous reality. You are beyond the speed of light.

The frequencies of unified Consciousness have maximum power and amplitude. The high amplitude power permeates all the dimensions and delivers a most palpable experience of Source. In this understanding, you are constantly entrained by your own evolution. You are living a Sourceful experience that is more powerful than your mind or any of the dimensions below it. Within that Sourceful experience, the data of all the dimensions shifts from fragmentation and illusion to unified Consciousness and wholeness. But, again, it is experiential not conceptual.

You might say it's the experience before the concept; the concept may still be there, but it very quickly diminishes in relation to the experience. Such is the progressive evolutionary process of an ever-increasing integrative wholeness. There is no doing. It is rather Being. Doing is illusion. Being is wholeness. It is simply the integrative flow of Consciousness. That's what synchronicity really means, "the integrative flow of one Consciousness," that's the synchronicity experience.

Hallelujah

Continuing Expansion After Awakening

While it is occurring to me, I want to ask you about your current state of awareness, and is there a development that's happening in your consciousness?

What you're asking is, am I still evolving? Of course I am. Nothing stops. It is a great misunderstanding in the westernization of the Eastern traditions that enlightenment is the big finish. But that is totally antithetical to the evolution of Consciousness, which is forever expanding itself.

Therefore, enlightenment or wholeness is not a static point that you reach; it is rather a progressive experience that continues to evolve. While there is a point of constant unified Consciousness, where you have constant unified awareness, and yet thereafter it continues to evolve.

So it keeps on deepening forever.

Yes. I was very fortunate to have Muktananda as a Master because I could observe that process in him over the twelve years of our association. His wholeness evolved ever more subtle, day by day, until he was mostly light. That's exactly what happened: he got subtler and subtler and subtler, until he was just light. There was hardly any density left. He was so luminous he was transparent. His holistic power also exponentially increased.

And the subtler it gets, the more powerful it is. It is the same in my own experience. I have a consistent level of holistic experience and yet, day by day, I am more than I have ever been. Anyone can truthfully say that at any level of the journey. I invite people to affirm such each day: in every way, every day I am more than I have ever been. It is the truth of evolving Consciousness. I've grown through another day; I've evolved through another day. I am so much more than I have ever been. It is true for me. It is the progressive process of an ever-increasing integrative wholeness.

The Birth Of The Awakener Function

Okay. Let's go into the birth of the awakener function in you.

The awakener function is the role of the Master, but not everyone who experiences wholeness and the enlightening state of being is an awakener. It is a specific function inherent in your Consciousness. That is certainly true with me. Both the Divine Mother and Muktananda foretold that this was to be my role. It wasn't something I decided to do.

My own evolving experience was my consuming focus. Yet, I noticed that when I reached a certain level of holistic consistency, people around me experienced my entrainment. It happened before Muktananda, my own teacher, had moved on and left his body. But it was not my focus. I was with my teacher and that's exactly where I wanted to be. He gave me some very wise advice at the time. He said, "Try to keep secret as long as you can. Otherwise, they'll take every minute of your time. For your own delight in the experience, try to keep it to yourself as long as you can." So I remained within my own experience.

When he left his body and I came here to this very place in Virginia, it was with that intention. I just wanted to be by myself. I'd been in a very intense process for the previous twelve years and just wanted to be quiet and enjoy the experience I was experiencing, the suntan I had gotten. I lived simply and quietly in a little cottage on a rural farm with just a few close disciples living near by.

The guru principle gradually became active. This one would appear, and that one would appear, and people started to show up from here, there, and everywhere. I had maybe a year or so and then the number of disciples radically increased based on experiences they had when they met me, or because I'd appeared in their dreams or meditations. Thus the role sort of assumed me, and when it got to the point where I couldn't keep them away, without it being a detriment to their process, for my own more selfish interests in being alone, I surrendered to the experience whose time had come.

Emptiness Fullness: The Experience Of Giving "Shaktipat" In The Awakened State

I would like to ask you about transmission and Shaktipat. Can you tell me about what that experience is for you in the awakened state, and also about your contemporized high-tech version of this?

The experience that you term Shaktipat, which is a Sanskrit word for empowerment, Grace, or Kundalini awakening, or the energetic transmission from the Master to the disciple that awakens the disciple, is from the Tantric tradition. It is very thorough in its delineation of the guru principle, the necessity of the guru, and the mark of the true guru as the one who not only has the power to awaken Kundalini, but further, is masterful enough to guide that awakened Kundalini to the culmination of its journey in wholeness, or the enlightening state. It is the mark of the authentic guru and cannot be faked. In Tantric understanding, it is determined by God and the guru and is therefore the Grace-bestowing power of the divine.

Of course, my teacher Muktananda was very well known for his awakening power. He was a "Johnny Appleseed" of awakening in the West, awakening thousands of people, which was unusual. Most gurus awaken a few people, have a few disciples and guide them very specifically in their journey. He rather awakened the masses by the thousands. He also had a few close disciples whom he groomed, guiding that awakening to its fullness and culmination.

In my case, he very thoroughly educated me in the awakening process and made me his ambassador. I functioned as a representative through which his awakening power flowed. Yet, he told me that in this way I would have the experience and understand the mechanics and that one day the awakening power would come to me. And that's what happened as I moved around the world as an ambassador for him, giving that initiation, that Shaktipat, to thousands of people. Then it came to me and continued after he made his transition.

In the early years, it wasn't a specific focus. I didn't give programs where I specifically focused on empowerment or Shaktipat, but people would meet me, and spontaneously experience classical Kundalini awakening. Over time, it became a formalized focused empowerment experience.

People had to be educated about it what was, in the West especially, where they are particularly naive about these aspects of spiritual/mystical experience. So I created a context in which it could be explained as well as offered as an experience, as an awakening initiation. Yet, I wanted to deliver it in a contemporary way, because Muktananda had instructed me to contemporize this ancient mystical knowledge that he had taught, and to create a new and modern context for it. It required a modern context for the West that would be easier for people to relate to, based on their enculturation.

The experience of Shaktipat became the experience of contemporary empowerment, and I created a technological context of empowerment that is known as the Synchronicity High-Tech Empowerment, offered here at the Synchronicity Sanctuary. People who come here for retreats are given the option of this experience and of course it's in great demand because of its rarity.

My experience of it is very simple: I've been on both sides. I was a disciple to a Shaktipat guru and I know what the experience is, and what it causes, and all the unfoldment of it, from its awakening to its culmination under the guidance of an adept.

Now that I am on the Master's side, I know also what the experience is for the Master. The best way I can describe the experience of empowerment or transmission for the Master is emptiness. I have a little sign in the control room where I sit that always reminds me, and its two words are "emptiness/fullness." What this means to me is, "if I am empty, they are full." I must elevate to the subtlest level of my being, to absorption in Being, and remain elevated in absolute emptiness and stillness.

It is an energetic flow that seems to just flow through you. You become the focal point of a power that is amplified and moves through you, eliciting that awakening and expansion of awareness, expanding, entraining, elevating experience in the disciple. The perspective I would embrace here is: emptiness/fullness is the Master's motto on empowerment.

That's beautiful. Thank you

Quantum Physics: A New Language Of Awakening

You employ the language of quantum physics to create a bridge between mystical experience and the modern mind. Would you speak about how that evolved and why you feel it's important? What is the value that you see in it?

Muktananda's request was that I find a way to westernize, to update the ancient, time-honored, mystical truth. He said that I specifically should do this because I was an American and a Westerner. As a dutiful disciple, I endeavored to impeccably follow the direction of my Master.

I began with simplification and translation in order to build a bridge from East to West. I eliminated all of the unnecessary cultural trappings that surrounded the pure mystical truth that could be an obstacle to Western people. If the holistic model was based on their Western enculturation, it would minimize resistance and be more easily understandable. I translated everything into English, eliminating the use of so much of the Sanskrit language.

At the same I also recognized that science is the basis of Western enculturation. We are educated from our earliest years in a scientific paradigm, and therefore more easily comprehend when things are presented in a scientific context. I continued my exploration of the cutting edge of modern science, which was the new physics and quantum mechanics. What did these modern sciences have to say about the nature of reality, and how did it compare to the ten thousand year old mystical revelations of the Tantra? There needed to be a marriage of the two, a merging of the two and that was my intention.

This merging was already operative in a number of notable western scientists who had more mystical/spiritual experience. When Muktananda came to the United States he met many scientists who were intrigued by his state of being, and the experience that he catalyzed in them. There was a whole group of Berkeley and Stanford scientists who had ongoing dialogues with Muktananda. Their intention was to intellectually reframe the experience based on their own scientific understanding.

I was included in these dialogues and learned that the cutting edge of modern science was saying exactly what the most ancient mystical/spiritual revelation on the planet had said about the nature of reality. In fact, the most recent update of the Tantra, which was Kashmir Shavism from the ninth through twelfth centuries, was even more specific in its agreement with modern science in terms of the nature of holistic reality.

The whole process of contemporization and westernization was an experience whose time had come. It was happening and I became part of it. When the Master tells you to do something, it magically unfolds and you must just flow with it. That was my experience in this regard. It just miraculously unfolded. It became what I termed the New Empirical Mysticism. It was the merging of the ancient and the modern, science and mysticism, into an updated and modern holistic model of reality. It also included modern technology.

Modern scientific technology had to be included because it too is a form of Consciousness. Separation is illusion. Consciousness diversifies itself in order to more fully experience itself. I had to say, well, this too is consciousness; you can't separate anything and you can't separate its technology out of it. If everything is consciousness creating itself in diversified and myriad forms through which it experiences itself ever more fully, well, I included technology as part of the holistic model of reality and the mechanics of its actualization in human evolutionary experience.

I used the two hemispheres of the human brain as the microcosmic representation of relative reality. When they are imbalanced in function, there is fragmented experience. When balanced, there is holistic experience. Whole-brain synchrony is the scientific term used to describe the experience of unified Consciousness. The scientific principle of entrainment can be understood in relation to the human brain. Whether it is experienced by a Yogi ten thousand years ago in a Himalayan cave, or modern American today in a New York City apartment, it has the same effect. It can deliver the same precision meditation experience and the same states of unified Consciousness or wholeness. If you understand how the brain functions, and you understand brainwaves and brainwave patterns and frequencies consistent with holistic states of experience, then you could elicit that experience via the principle of entrainment.

So, I created Synchronicity High-Tech Meditation and began to experiment with it long before Muktananda had left his body. I subsequently created the modern holistic lifestyle that included technological meditation and made it available to people the world over. That was more than twenty years ago, and it has literally transformed the lives of hundreds of thousands of people. That means hundreds of thousands of people have had a precision meditative experience who otherwise might never have had one. It has put a lot of people on the meditator's seat and it has opened the doorway to the consideration of a new and modern version of reality.

Holistic models of reality, with one Consciousness as the Source, have been around for three hundred years since the Age of Idealism. There is agreement in scholarly circles, meaning that in most scholarly, academic, university circles, everybody agrees that the nature of reality, the true nature of reality, is holistic. There is only One and Consciousness is the substratum. Yet, the failure of those models is that they have never been translated into a lifestyle that the masses could experience on a daily basis.

What I endeavored to do was to create the holistic lifestyle that would actualize the model. The Synchronicity community has lived the model and experientially validated it for over twenty years. We have been acknowledged by our peers in that not only did we intellectually embrace a holistic model of reality, but we validated it through our experience and created a context through which it could be shared with others for further validation. Thus, it includes the three principles of authentic science: you have a paradigm or a model, you prove it, and then you offer it to others for validation/invalidation.

In this understanding, we have truthfully actualized the Synchronicity Experience and I think it's important that it be mentioned. We receive grateful acknowledgement from our peers and from the world population that we have inspired. In this understanding, why would all these people stay with it? It's obviously not just a fad. It has continued for over twenty years and just keeps growing. The bottom line is, it works. If you have an authentic legitimate experience of balance and wholeness, well of course you are going to stay with it. That's the brilliance of the Synchronicity Experience: it works, it delivers.

Music, Sound, And Source

When did your interest in music begin, and was it influenced by the mystical experiences that you were having? Did they interplay with each other at an early age? They obviously do so now, and I'm wondering, what was that interplay?

They did interplay at an early age. I liked religious music and sang in the choir. I was an altar boy and I liked the High Mass because the associated sounds reminded me of the sounds that I heard in my more mystical moments. So the first music I explored was religious in nature. In addition to religious music, I also studied music at school and at home. Also, my older sister was learning to play the piano.

I was surrounded by music in my formative years and took the opportunity to learn all about it. Through my teenage years, I progressed to the enculturated sounds of the day and moved from the slow, ethereal and spiritual, religious sounds. With the advent of Muktananda, I moved back into the mystical, and all the Eastern cultural music and subsequent exploration that unfolded. The Synchronicity music is the result of it all.

So it was after meeting Muktananda, that the Synchronicity sound technology and the Synchronicity Paradigm were born?

Yes, the Synchronicity Experience and its technology were really born during the Muktananda years, because surrounding Muktananda was a very eclectic and unique audience that included many notable authors, intellectuals, scientists, and people from diverse cultural backgrounds.

One of them was a man named Itzhak Bentov. He wrote a book called Stalking the Wild Pendulum. We had many conversations, and his more Western scientific way of explaining Consciousness and the nature of reality was very exciting to me as a direction. Basically, it's all about relative reality and the polarization of consciousness. The roots of the Synchronicity Experience go all the way back to the early 1970s; the development of the musical aspect of Synchronicity also goes back to those days with Muktananda and the different sounds of chant and mantra.

The education that I received in the mechanics of how music and sound affect human Consciousness was invaluable. The majority of its components were evolved during the Muktananda years. He was very instrumental in all of it: giving me musical instruments to play, encouraging me, educating me, mentoring me in every possible way. Then after he died and I settled here in Virginia where I had the time to focus on it, I put it all together into what is now the Synchronicity Experience. But it certainly finds its roots – I mean, it's got a bit of everything in it – from my earliest years up to the present. In all, it includes the whole of my life experience.

Were there other specific influences that were key in that process?

Many notable people came and went from that group, including Carlos Castaneda, Edgar Mitchell the astronaut, and a lot of university people and people from the creative arts. Muktananda spent a lot of time in Northern California, so there were many scientists, medical doctors, psychiatrists, psychologists etc.

Were there moments during those times when you were thinking, "Aha! This can be put into technology; this can be used to assist in the transformational process?"

Yes, absolutely. The Synchronicity technology emerges from the study of the nature of Consciousness within relative reality. Analyzed at the vibrational energetics of the traditional Eastern yogi in his hand-cut cave and how that impacted a human being, as compared to other geometrics like the experience of a meditator in a square apartment in New York City, or in a rectangular home in the suburbs.

Bhagavan Nityananda apparently carved many caves himself with his own hands out of stone, so people could meditate.

Yes. The focus of my study was just looking at the energetic experience in there, the focus becomes: how does one's environment, one's surroundings, affect one's Consciousness?

The result of that study was the understanding of the oscillation of polarity, the frequencies of vibration and their correspondences to the brainwaves of the bicameral human being. It involves the principle of entrainment, and the mechanics of creating an environment that is a modern cave.

Thus, when you were away from the Master, who was the most powerful entrainment, you could utilize everything available to you at the cutting edge of Consciousness to replicate that entrainment. That was the intention: How do I bring the cave into the 21st century? How do I make meditation modern so that more people can embrace it? Remember, these were the 70's and meditation in Western culture was considered the work of the devil. I mean, it was not highly regarded and few people practiced it.

Therefore, I was looking for ways to make it Western and modern, and to help people understand it and make it more acceptable. To these ends, I also included modern science. This is the progressive development that the Divine Mother always told me about, saying "Experience everything. It's all preparation and one day you'll understand." When I finally settled in Virginia and created the Synchronicity Experience, I really began to see the kaleidoscope come together.

Over the past twenty years, I've watched the refining of that paradigm and the clarifying of it in a way that can be precisely presented and actualized as an experience by the average Western person in the midst of their modern 21st-century life. I stay on the cutting edge of evolving technology in the understanding that Consciousness has but one intention; to be fully itself.

Therefore, it's constantly manifesting more and more of itself, and why wouldn't Consciousness utilize all that it is to fully experience itself? Science, technology, and whatever else is available is but a form of Consciousness, so we must harness it to have a more comprehensive experience of ourselves as Consciousness. It's just a validation of the primary intention in Consciousness, which is to fully be itself.

The Synchronicity Paradigm: Balance Yields Wholeness

In the synchronicity paradigm you emphasize the relationship between the body, mind, and emotions, and point out the benefit in balancing those three dimensions to yield greater access to mystical awareness?

The Synchronicity Paradigm has two major components, the holistic model of reality and the holistic lifestyle that actualizes the model. The holistic lifestyle also has two components — contemporary high-tech meditation, which is the technological form of meditation used because of its precision, and conscious life-affirmative living.

The Synchronicity holistic model of reality is based on the Tantric holistic model of reality as updated in Kashmir Shaivism, and further updated in conjunction with modern science and Western enculturation. It is cutting edge, yet we can trace its roots back ten thousand years.

The most essential point is that holistic reality means that the nature of reality is One. One Consciousness is the Source or the substratum of a multidimensional reality, from subtle to dense. We can observe the One multi-dimensional Consciousness from subtle to dense both in the universal macrocosm and in the individual microcosm.

In human experience, from dense to subtle, the dimensions are: physical, emotional, mental, subtle, causal and supra-causal. These six dimensions are governed by relative reality, which is the arena of all experience. The densest of these dimensions are the most challenging because we are very identified with the body, the emotions and the mind. In the Synchronicity Paradigm I term it the Primary Trinity – the physical, the emotional and the mental dimensions. The relative polarities therein are the most imbalanced.

Consciousness is the most fragmented in those dimensions and that is where humans have the most illusory experience of duality and separation. Here, the basic assumption is: I am separate and different from my world and from everyone else. The subject is perceived as fundamentally separate and different from the object, which of course is illusion.

But in the densest dimensions, because they're so imbalanced, and because the oscillation of polarities is so slow, it is easy to experience that illusion and that seeming separation. Therefore, in order to experience the subtle dimensions – which only actualize based on balance in the denser dimensions – it is imperative to first walk where your feet are. That is, first bring balance to the denser dimensions, the physical, emotional, and mental.

When the Primary Trinity is balanced in duration and harmonically coherent as a result, the subtle dimensions actualize. Therefore, if you want to have the experience of unified Consciousness and wholeness – holistic experience – you must actualize the subtle dimensions.

But you can't actualize them until you have balanced the denser foundation beneath them. The analogy I use is this: it's great to build a skyscraper, because you can take the elevator to the top floor and get the 360-degree panoramic view. But, if you haven't built a solid foundation, when you take the elevator to the top, the building will wobble and fall down. Likewise, without a balanced foundation, you cannot sustain holistic experience.

Thus, the Primary Trinity is the starting point for everyone in the evolution of their Consciousness, and we place great emphasis on it within the Synchronicity Experience. We must first learn how to balance the physical, emotional and mental dimensions, and progressively develop the consistency of that balance so that it becomes harmonically coherent, and then the subtle dimensions automatically and naturally actualize as a result. Holistic experience, which is proportional to balance, then becomes consistent in your experience. That's what the Synchronicity Experience is, the integrative flow of one unified Consciousness.

Our Self-Destructive Human Game From The Viewpoint Of Enlightening Awareness

I would like to ask you about our planet. You spoke about the Divine Mother, and it strikes me that, as a human race, we are destroying our earthly mother at a rapid clip. People are suffering as a result of such a frantic pace of life. How would you address this from the viewpoint of holistic awareness?

From the viewpoint of a holistic awareness, consistent within the experience of a unified consciousness, everything is exactly the way it's supposed to be. Unified Consciousness simply observes its play and says "I manifested myself that I might ever more fully experience myself, and all experience is valid. This is my play and I am experiencing the experience I intended, so there's nothing wrong, there's nothing right, it is as it is and as it is not. It is appropriate."

Yet, this perspective is confined to less than five percent of the human population according to current sociological statistics. The remaining 95 percent have quite a different perspective, because they don't have a unified experience, a holistic experience. The majority of the human population is fragmented. They have freewill and are at choice. Based on their choices, so is their life experience; what they choose is what they get.

The current world around us has resulted from the choices of the collective consciousness, and the choices of the collective consciousness are either life-negative and fear-based, or life-affirmative and love-based. The two polarities are still operative at any level of relative reality: whether it's subtle or dense, the same polarities are operative. In the densest levels, where 95 percent of the population is mired, these are the choices.

The negative polarity is dominant and thus the choices of the collective consciousness are particularly life-negative and fear-based. Their experience is imbalanced and fragmented. They're imbalanced that way, and therefore, what do we see? We see the negation of life. In any context, from the environment, to politics, to nations, you see the same experience. The question is: why is their choice what it is? The answer is that individual and collective Consciousness is evolving itself through all experience.

Consciousness, in whatever form, at whatever level of evolution, evolves its wholeness through its choices and correspondent experiences. In truth, much is at stake in the choices that everyone makes. What's at stake? The evolution of your Consciousness.

It is through our experience that we learn, we grow and we evolve in wholeness. We must therefore be wakeful in our choices, because what we choose is what we experience. If we choose life negation and fear, destruction and violence, this is what we manifest as our experience both individually and collectively. Yet, we have to have that experience or otherwise, how will we know it? How will we learn it? On the one hand we abhor it; on the other hand, we say, "Wait a minute, maybe it's necessary. If the experience is horrible enough, I might consider changing it. Maybe I need a certain amount of that experience; maybe I have to get really a full dose full of the misery of life before I choose to change it into the celebration of life. Perhaps I can change my suffering into celebration."

Consciousness always presents this choice. Look at all the diversity of experience on this planet; it is Consciousness diversified. Look at every nation, every race, all the different modes of experience and expression that people are having on this planet, and be aware that the intention in Consciousness is simply to observe and experience both its unity and diversity.

So shouldn't it be, "Well, let's sit down and share your experience, everybody's experience, and see how each one is a different facet of the same consciousness, a different experience of the same One, a diversified perspective that makes us all more?" In truthful awareness, we would share our experience and delight in the diversity of our unity. That's the truthful intention operative in Consciousness. But as it makes itself more dense and forfeits that awareness, what do we find? We find people who don't share, people who are isolated, people who are polarized, people who are marginalized, people who are discriminative and bigots. We find the illusion of separation, all that basically says: "you and I are separate and different, and there's nothing to share. My way is better than your way. Do what I say or I'll kill you!" That's the densest level of experience.

The important message is: look at your choices. Through your choices, you live. You are here to evolve. The majority experience on this planet today is very primitive. We're not very evolved in Consciousness based on the choices we make when we so easily pick up a gun and shoot another person to death who doesn't agree with us.

This is radical fragmentation in Consciousness, and that only five percent of our human population has any holistic experience, any unified experience, says a lot about us as a human race. Yet, from the truthful perspective of that five percent, it's all appropriate, because all experience is valid. I can't sit here and judge anybody's experience and say it's inappropriate. It isn't. Based on their model of reality and where they are in the evolution of individuated Consciousness, the experience they are choosing is appropriate for them or it wouldn't be happening.

I have to honor everyone's experience. I can agree to disagree, and I don't have to choose the same experience for myself, but I have no right to invalidate anybody else's experience. That is holistic perspective. It says: The truth is, there is only One; everything is a play of Consciousness. In all the dimensions of its experience, Consciousness is evolving itself appropriately for its own delight, for its own entertainment, for the joy of the experience.

What is important for me is to take responsibility for myself, to be aware of where my feet are, and what choices I'm making in order that I maximize the evolution of my soul and deliver myself to increasingly integrated states of wholeness and unified consciousness. In this way, I will make a truthful contribution to my world.

Hallelujah!

Dr Richard Moss

Introduction
Embodying Consciousness In Relationship

Richard Moss is an M.D., an intrepid explorer of consciousness, and a person of profound intellect who embodies a deep compassion. After undergoing a spontaneous mystical awakening on his thirtieth birthday, Richard left his medical practice to explore working with groups of people interested in opening to more profound levels of aliveness and relatedness. For Richard, *the word Consciousness is synonymous with the word Relationship*, an insight that is at the core of his teaching and his awakening.

Wondrously, a short while after Richard's initial energetic opening, during a period of retreat at a friend's home while sitting in the garden, Richard observed two butterflies mating, a black one and a white one. When they ended their merry dance and parted, one of the butterflies (the black one) flew toward Richard and alighted on his forehead. At that precise moment, the energetic opening that had taken hold of his being a few months earlier, exploded into the fullness of divine realization, or what Richard refers to as Fundamental Realization. A full description of this event is given in Richard's book, *The Black Butterfly*. Nine months after this awakening Richard was to undergo another significant quickening within his consciousness while on retreat in India, where he found himself falling backwards through time and simultaneously forward, into the womb of the eternal feminine. This is described in Richard's book, *The I That Is We*. Richard has explored and deepened his awakening through the medium of his own life and relationships, and also through his spiritual work with groups of people, many of whom are drawn to him during periods of great illness. This work with groups continues to be the field of his own ongoing spiritual unfoldment and deepening embodiment of consciousness.

My first introduction to Richard Moss came many years ago in Melbourne, Australia. Not too long after my own energetic opening, I came across Richard's work and shortly thereafter was delighted to discover he was due to be visiting Australia to give a series of talks and retreats. I was fortunate to be able to attend a retreat, where I was moved by his deep honesty. During his talks I repeatedly experienced the sense that the intelligence of Nature itself, was operating through Richard as he spoke to us of the potential shift in consciousness that is imminent *within us*, and unfolding *through us* — a shift that Richard describes as a *deepening of our capacity for relationship*. As I listened, I was infused with a sense of mystery and awe with regards to the vast majesty and intelligence of Nature.

During the talk I attempted to open myself fully to the potent energy of such a group dynamic, yet I found myself being burnt out rather than inwardly renewed, my nervous system fried. This, I would discover, was due to my own naive insistence that I always remain in the most expanded state. I would later learn through Richard's work that we need to allow the natural ebb and flow of the awakened current, giving equal space to the high tide of expansion *and* the low tide of rest, wherein the intensity of energy seems to diminish. Over the years this insight has granted a great freedom, and has flowered into an increasing recognition of the silent background, the simple sense of Presence that supports all states and movements in consciousness.

During this retreat I was blessed to meet a woman named Alia, who would become a friend and who, as it happened, was a friend of Richard's and a long-time student of his work. Alia was suffering from terminal cancer. Yet, over time, I came to see that Alia embodied a deep level of radiant aliveness, and was sustaining her rapidly declining physical form through her transparency to the larger Field of Being, which infused her ailing body with life force.

Dr Richard Moss

I am moved to share a little story from my time with Alia as an example of what it means to live in faith and in surrender to life as a lover, even in the midst of profound pain, suffering, and imminent death. On a beautiful summer's day in Byron Bay, Alia offered to take me for a drive into the mountains. She wanted to show me a particular river that she liked. Keep in mind during this story that Alia's cancer was so advanced that sneezing would break her ribs; in fact, broken bones in her fragile body were the norm. Her companion was a moderately healthy, able-bodied young man.

So there we were, winding our way up the mountain, speeding along narrow dirt roads, leaving trails of dust behind us. I was amazed at Alia's zest for driving at such speed in her state of ill health. Soon we came upon the place she had spoken of. The car pulled up and Alia jumped out with all the vigour and zest of a child. And to my total surprise, the next thing I knew she had leapt off a steep cliff that was studded with rocks and trees, and was calling out for me to follow her. I was amazed and stunned that in her ailing body there was infinitely more energy and love of life than I was accustomed to in my own apparent good health. Alia's embrace of life was a sheer delight to behold. I felt her every movement as an invitation to say YES to what is, to greet life as a lover. I scurried over to the cliff, stumbling as I put on my shoes, not wanting to hurt my feet on the rocky ground. As I approached the steep decline, I was dumbfounded to see Alia already at the bottom. She had somehow made her way out into the centre of a swiftly flowing river and was now perched on a slippery rock, from where she was calling, "Come and see the eel playing about in the water!" Well, let me tell you – I stumbled down that hill, hanging onto the tree branches for dear life, nearly slipping several times, even with my protective shoes on. I felt in my heart the stark contrast between Alia's open fluidity and trust in her body, and my own halting movements, my calculating mind, and stiff rigid body.

The reason I share this story is, firstly, that it was one of the deepest experiential lessons of my life; secondly, it perfectly illustrates what I consider to be the essence of Richard's work and orientation to life. Like each of the beautiful human beings in this book, Richard is a kind of Tantric master, a master of the *conscious embrace*, deeply affirming all of life as inherently Divine. His mantra, if he has one, appears to be simply "YES." Apart from his depth of insight and spiritual maturity, Richard's greatest gift is his unfailing ability to inspire us to say "Yes" to life.

I was deeply honored to receive Richard's *Yes* in response to my invitation to take part in this project, and am excited to share this interview with you.

During my stay in Ojai I was to be bedding down on a rustic farm nestled away in the Ojai suburbs, surrounded by mountains sacred to the Cherokee Indians. The sun filled all and everything with the vibrancy of life as birds played in the air and dogs barked happily in the background, letting me know I was once again back in suburbia. On the second day of my stay, after a good night's rest, Richard generously arrived to pick me up for the interview which was to take place at his home.

The Breakdown Of The Perceptual Matrix

Okay, so how many years ago was it now, that this change in your state of consciousness that you speak about, took place?

It was 1977. I was 30.

What was occupying your consciousness in that general period of your life?

When I looked back at the time and asked myself, "Why did this happen to me?" I thought about it in many different terms. But one scientific model that could act as a metaphor is the notion for which Ilya Prigogine got the Nobel Prize. It was his dissipative structures concept, which says that certain systems, when you add energy to them, will break down and degenerate into chaos, while other systems will organize into a way of handling more energy than before. So, a new pattern emerges that can handle much more energy than before. At least, that was my way of understanding it...

I had been living at full tilt. I was doing emergency-room medicine, and clinical adult medicine, in my clinic and at a hospital. If I wasn't doing some kind of spiritual retreat or inquiry, I'd be rushing off to rock climb whenever I had free time. I was part of an organization called Seekers After Truth, and we were doing work that was related to Ichazo, Gurdjieff, Vipassana, and a whole bunch of things. I had finished an intensive process of family self-inquiry, which now is called The Hoffman Process – at the time it was called The Fischer-Hoffman Process – and was being taught by Bob Hoffman and a few people that he trained. It was about a six-month process that involved, oh, at least ten to twenty hours a week of writing and work. And there I was doing emergency-room medicine and climbing. In 1975 I'd gone to Peru, and for the first time had done real high-altitude mountaineering in some very challenging and dangerous conditions that took me to the physical limits of myself. So I was at a peak level, physically. I was also using my mind, intensely and fully. I was seeking in the age-old sense of seeking to know myself, seeking to understand the deeper mysteries. And I was engaged in a work that I knew was never going to be my lifetime career, but which was, nevertheless, quite challenging, and where I would often put in long hours. And I was doing significant rebuilding and remodelling of my own house, as well as beginning to develop a few rental properties. So my life was amazingly full, and then this transformational experience or awakening process just "happened."

Actually, I never sought after it. I didn't have within my model that some specific experience might happen that would change me. I hadn't read enough or thought enough about that possibility. I had really no awareness of people like Ramana Maharshi or Nisargadatta or Ramakrishna, or Aurobindo, or any of the Indian sages; that came later. But I was reading the *Yoga Sutras* of Patanjali. I was studying the sutras and meditating in the mornings, for a few hours, and going to the clinic, or doing what I was doing. Some of this input I understood but mostly, I really didn't understand.

The actual experience that happened was simply – or not so simply – a breakdown of my perceptual matrix; first, a loss of boundary, a sense of merging with everything, which I at first found very frightening. The "me" consciousness wasn't so much surrendering as it was being overwhelmed, in the way in which a drug experience might overwhelm it, but this was not related to any drug experience.

This experience was going on for a few days. And right at that time, I had the chance to meet Franklin Merrell-Wolff – a man of realization, a Western sage. I would describe him as a western version of someone like Ramana Maharshi. You can read him: *Pathways Through to Space* and *The*

Philosophy of Consciousness Without An Object are his two principal books. He also gave many talks on tape. He was an old man of 89 when I met him. In fact, I met him on the day that this perceptual breakdown started. Seeking to understand what was going on, I asked myself a question: "Is this phenomenological in the sense of *medical?*" And based on my medical background, it couldn't be explained. What I was experiencing couldn't be explained as psychosis; it wasn't a seizure; there was no explanation. The next basic question actually came from a sudden realization. While I wasn't Christian, or religious, just before this happened, maybe a month before, I had carefully read the Gospels, and for some reason they'd had a very powerful impacted on me. I cried. There was a lot of recognition and I didn't know why. I was really so deeply moved.

I could say that for a year before this event, there was a very strong sense of foreshadowing, in the sense that I just kept feeling like "What am I alive for? There's no reason to be alive." There was a despair. Even though I was doing all these things, it all seemed very meaningless to me. It didn't seem real. It was real when someone was suffering; it was real when I was working with someone in the emergency room. But my life seemed so unreal to me. The climbing, which was somewhat before that, was of course very real. But what seemed unreal to me was why I even put myself in that experience – why was I pushing my edges that way? So when this unexplainable experience came, I said to myself, "Okay, if I can't explain this, then I will simply observe what's happening in my mind.'" And I went into an intense process of saying, "This is a thought (as a thought came into my mind)…this is a feeling (as I observed a feeling,) here is another thought…." And when I say intense, I mean it's the only thing I did.

The perceptual process had broken down, and it went on for days. I was unable to sleep – there was so much energy moving through me. I was just unable to sleep. Along the way I realized that every thought created a feeling. Every thought created an emotion. Every emotion created a thought. I had to disengage thought from emotion: I knew that. I don't know how I knew it. And then I had a vision that Jesus had realized this state. Someone had come before me. I didn't have any background in Buddhism, or Hinduism, or any threads of mysticism that I had paid much attention to. Only Walt Whitman's poetry. So I said to myself, "Well, if Jesus has lived through this, then I understand that consciousness is perpetual... uninterrupted, and available to me." So, I had the insight: I have to realize that consciousness. Whatever that consciousness was, I had to realize it. That's when the inquiry process started.

Fundamental Realization: The Absolute Perfection And Rightness Of All Things

I said, "Okay, if I have to realize a consciousness I don't know, let me begin by identifying a consciousness that I do know.'" So, it didn't matter what the thought was – whether it was spiritually oriented or fear-oriented, or the emotion, the anxiety about what was happening to me – because it was very, very, ... challenging. Perhaps I owe my ability to have gone through that experience because I had faced difficult challenges before, going through medical training and as a climber. I had a very well developed will power. But on the other hand maybe it was so challenging because I was so well developed in my mind. And my mind wanted to understand and control everything. But the recognition that a new consciousness couldn't be the one I knew, meant that I just simply said, "That's a thought. That's a feeling. That's an emotion. That's a sensation." And I just did that on and on.

I continued like this for days and nights, getting a little bit of rest from time to time. And I had the support of a wonderful wise woman, who trusted that what I was experiencing was not mental illness, but some kind of profound psychic opening. She was a Jungian psychoanalyst, and she recognized it immediately as something not within the normal range of anxiety. And so she took me to her home, and created in it a kind of sacred space for me, and cancelled her other work, and left me alone but stayed available. It was at her home that I was doing this process: "This is a thought. This is an emotion. This is a thought that's creating an emotion. This is an emotion that's inviting a thought. This is sensation. This is perception." Just doing it – emptying myself – just, "This is, not a consciousness I don't know. This is a consciousness I do know."gg And that's when I observed, suddenly, these two butterflies dancing in the air… and then landing on a branch, just above me, and… mating… and then parting from the mating… and the black one landed on my forehead.

When it landed on my forehead, my mind just…went empty. Suddenly, where there had been days and days of deep disturbance, there was silence. And then gradually the silence became joy. And the joy became a recognition of relationship and oneness with everything, the absolute perfection and rightness of all things. I realized that everything is perfect, and had always been perfect.

This went on for the rest of that day, from early in the morning all through the day. That evening, my friend put on "The Hallelujah Chorus," along with the rest of Handel's *Messiah*. I lay down and listened to the music … and suddenly, I had the imagery of what that music was about. The valleys – which are the fearful, low places of self-identification – they are lifted up; the mountains and hills – the inflation, the grandiosity, the self-importance – are made low. You have to "make in the desert a highway for God." And I realized that there was an ancient tradition – an ancient understanding – of doing exactly what I had done by eliminating identification with thought, sensation, emotion, and feeling.

I realized that the song – all the music – was about what was happening to me. "And who shall stand when He appears in the whole of His light, like refiner's fire?" So, whereas *The Messiah* is taken from lines from Isaiah and other prophets, it was speaking directly to me about the experience that I was having, and it was the experience of realizing whatever you want to call it. But in my process it was... I gave it a name at the time – it was Christ Consciousness – without any sense inside of me that I was Christ, or anything of the sort. I also intuitively and instinctually knew that that was a universal consciousness, that it was available to everyone, that it was rarely realized, and that Christianity, and almost every offshoot of that original realization, of that original consciousness, was an interpretation by the old consciousness. It was a misinterpretation, in that most of what we read, and most of what we hear in conventional religion is ordinary consciousness trying to understand a different dimension... that it has not yet experienced.

The Birth Of A New Sensitivity To Energy

So, I already knew how to see and sense and feel energy fields. I had been aware of energy – I had been taught about that, for a few years, through another teacher of mine, Brugh Joy. I could sense energy fields. I could scan the body for abnormalities in energy fields. I was aware of that. But I didn't understand what it was like to be one with everything, connected with everything. After that butterfly experience, the energy awareness was even stronger. I could feel people's minds move. I could not read their minds, but it seemed that what I said was an extension of what they were thinking.

I also saw that when I was the most vulnerable and my heart was broken open, and I reached toward where the other was, to acknowledge to them where they were, that it had an incredibly profound effect upon people... that it literally just opened their hearts. They fell in love. And so they began to study with me.

But it only worked that way if I was not involved with me. If I was afraid for me, if I was worried about me, if I wanted attention on me, if I wanted to place the emphasis on my process, and how disturbing it was and how difficult it was, then people were willing to listen and people were very interested, but the actual effect of what it awakened in me was not transferred to another.

One time I looked at a woman who was a secretary at a place where this "wise woman" friend of mine did some of her work and as I was walking past her, I suddenly realized how much work she did. I looked at her and I said, "Oh, man! You save her a lot, you answer the phone, you're an intermediary with so many people, and you really go unseen most of the time," and she just started to cry. I saw her a few weeks later when I was doing some sort of a weekend talk, because I had already begun to do a little bit of teaching, and she told me that she was just so flooded by love at the time that she didn't know what had happened to her. And she thought it had come from me. I told her that it was the same love in her that was in me. These are some of the elements of that experience.

I've written about walking to the edge of the cliffs where this woman's home was, the day after the butterfly landed on my forehead, and looking down and seeing a whale swimming in relatively shallow water. I could also see a boat, which was a whale-watching boat, about another hundred yards or so offshore from this whale, and I could see where the wake had come, all the way from the horizon straight in to that point, at that cliff, which was very near the house where I'd had the black butterfly experience. And I had the distinct feeling that the whale had been attracted by the consciousness I had entered. It occurred to me that cetaceans, perhaps because they don't have prehensile hands for "doing," are so very much in unitive consciousness – or what we human beings experience as unitive consciousness – that they recognize that consciousness. And maybe they even hold that consciousness on the planet for us, to some extent, and help enable our recognition of that consciousness. I just had the feeling that that creature, that being, had come to meet me – come as close as it could – to meet me. And that I had come to meet it.

I felt kindred-ness with life. I felt, as I walked past homes, the happiness and the unhappiness – mostly unhappiness – in almost all of them. I felt the incredible suffocation of women within their worlds, and the conflict of relationship. I just felt it – I sensed it. I knew it was hiding, but surely there, in so much of our world. I could feel it, just going down the street. I'd pass in front of a house, and I'd feel pain. I'd go in front of another house and I'd feel a different kind of pain, or a similar pain, and I'd walk past a house and I could almost hear the people fighting. I didn't know these people and I suppose I could write it off as simply projection, my projections on them. But in any case, it was a paranormal sensitivity, and it was very hard to live with for a long time. Certain places were especially difficult: airports were difficult, driving a car was difficult for me; I spent a lot of time walking, for hours at a time and this was true for several years.

In nature?

Primarily in nature. I also used to go along the roads, picking up litter, just to give myself something to do that was of service and at the same time keep me outdoors. I didn't go on roads that had a lot of traffic and were smelly. But you know, just the two-way roads, and the hills of Berkeley and Oakland. I learned to find my way back to the inner stillness through my voice, through singing, through chanting…through prayer…through dancing… through walking… specifically through walking at a particular speed, which was walking at the exact speed that allowed the maximum sensitivity to everything around me, and to the space of myself. So, not walking to get to anywhere in particular, but just walking, and finding the speed where I was walking as my life. And all of those experiences, those early experiences, of going between the old "me" and the new me, became the basis of many of the activities that I use in my teaching.

Even though I've had that experience, and thought about it so many times, it's so hard to speak about it accurately. I was really travelling in no man's land at the time. Until the black butterfly, it was very frightening and afterwards I had a long period of feeling nearly overwhelmed a lot of the time. It has given me a great deal of empathy for the fear that we have of annihilation, which is an aspect of mystical awakening.

Bringing Awakening Into Every Aspect Of Life

What can you say about the dissolution of that sense of being separate? As it unfolded in your journey, that is.

Well, it was coming home. It changed me forever. But I don't want to romanticize anything. I can look back, and I can see the strength of my mind – I wanted to understand, I wanted to be in control. That's the first miracle of consciousness – the consciousness of "me" that I often refer to these days as "me world." That me, the separate self is much too small, and feels when it moves into that other consciousness as if it's being threatened with annihilation.

I think we all have spontaneous openings – suddenly we're overwhelmed with love, suddenly we're filled with joy. To me, the expansive part of the opening is only the first half. After expansion there comes a "shadow – whatever has been repressed or buried in the consciousness – that has to come forward and be integrated into that love. For me that shadow was fear and distrust. I think that the original formation of "me" consciousness is achieved by burying so much, repressing so much, denying so much. We deny fear, we deny helplessness, we deny meaninglessness, we deny the full extent of our narcissistic desire to be

God, to be the universe. Even though it's running around there, in our subconscious, this self-involvement, this self-importance remains buried. But once we have opened and seen the light, I call it the "ascending process," then we have to start the descent and integrate what was buried. The need for integration isn't a choice, it is demanded of us whether we want it or feel ready or not.

Of course, to the extent that there's identification with "me," these darker energies are terrible: you oscillate between desolation, dissolution, and a sense of loss of self. But then, if you surrender deeply enough, you are once again established in emptiness-fullness, and there is a sense of joy, a sense of unity, a sense of completeness. Not that you deserve it, but that state re-establishes itself after each descent. And then, once again, consciousness starts to again identify with its former construction of "me" or "I" and we become too small for the process that is awakening in us. In our smallness, we are afraid so there is a sense of trying to put meaning into things, and a sense of trying to control things. And once again, that puts us into conflict, or friction, with this other larger impersonal energy, that IS, that requires nothing of us – no doing on our part. So once again we have to bring our minds fully into the now and surrender.

So, my experience was of swinging between "Richard" – who was too small for what he had awakened to – and a vast sense of being. When "I" was too small all this vast energy was energizing Richard's neurotic patterns, Richard's worries, giving them hundreds of times more force than normal. It was an unbearable state. More than unbearable; they were overwhelming. Therefore, they couldn't continue. Then there would be a cessation of struggle, and a return to deep calm. The struggle went on and on and on, and I began to watch it   watch it very carefully. And I watched what my assumptions were: my assumption was that bliss was freedom, unity was freedom, and that I was free and whole when in that state. My other basic assumption was that pain, fear, and anxiety were imprisonment, that I was failing, that there was something wrong with me when I felt these things. And I started to watch both of these assumptions as objects, so that I began to make straight in the desert a highway. I began to see that the awakening process cycles between high and low, expanded and contracted, and that who I really was, was both and neither.

In our ordinary consciousness we rarely touch the higher aspects of ourselves, but at the same time we rarely descend into the lower, more disturbing aspects of ourselves. Suddenly, when you awaken you get much bigger, and you can go up into truly expanded and extraordinary levels of perception, paranormal abilities, energy awareness, healing abilities, new perceptions… and then, then you go down into the hell realms, and the realms of real archetypal darkness, that are so annihilating to our first miracle – separate-self, ego consciousness. I found that that was my process.

My process was one of cycling, oscillating. If you drew it as a sine curve, you would see it going up and down. And now, after this awakening, it had much more amplitude; it would go much higher and much lower. If you think of it as a sphere, the sphere got bigger, and if I was in my heart – my heart would break open – then the dark and the light were integrated. They weren't in conflict with each other. But if my heart closed and I moved into my mind, then the dark and the light were antithetical, and in opposition.
And so when I was rejecting myself, or judging myself, or attempting to be free, I was right back in the state that was there before the black butterfly, with all this energy, but in an inadequate vehicle for that energy.

Do you mean an inadequate vehicle in the sense of just being deconstructed?

Well, our ego consciousness – this sense of separate self – is an inadequate vehicle for a larger perception of reality… a more complete perception of reality. And so the heart, as a centre, is really, as in Chinese medicine, an empty vessel that is filled by Spirit – by the universal Source. If the heart is open, then it naturally holds everything. That energy naturally in our bodies becomes male and female, positive and negative, you know, sodium and chloride, calcium and carbonate or sulphate. It becomes this dance of positive and negative... this dance of opposites, of polarities. And there's no conflict in that: it's all part of the expression of The One. But if there is conflict, if you are subconsciously choosing one over the other and you have a lot of energy, then it's hell.

So, I experienced myself creating hell, without intending to, just by re-identifying with "me," which is easy to do since that's all we've ever known since we were about three, four, or five years old. I guess our self-system is really intact by age five or six. That's what I call First Miracle Consciousness: the self-system, that makes us believe in this presumptive thing we call "me" or "I." along an energy that puts so much more energy into "me" or "I" that the me construct or the "I" can't sustain it. That was my experience.

I don't know whether that's really addressing the question. What I meant was that I cycled. Not in mania and depression, which are abnormal forms of cycling. But between despair and elation; between desolation and consolation. Saint Thomas Aquinas talks about the spiritual process or the spiritual path as being a movement between desolation and consolation. And different individuals seem to speak about that oscillation in different ways.

But for me it was basically that the dark had to be integrated into consciousness, and into the light. Dark as opposed to light, or light as opposed to dark, had to be integrated into something that was neither, something that was a deeper silence, a sort of deeper consciousness that could abide in ordinary life. In meditation, it's easy to reach a state where

I am integrated. It's in daily life... it's in relationship... it's in saying "yes" and saying "no" to people close to me, it's in setting boundaries, it's in being very precise and clear about what I want, knowing the other doesn't have to agree... It's in those areas that I find it's so easy to get small. And once you get small, then you're not a big enough vessel for your own realization.

And so then you go into desolation: you descend into darkness. But if your heart can open, then you're not only fit for relationship, you become a vessel for the deeper energy again, and there's a restoration of enthusiasm, and a sense of meaning, larger meaning. It's clarity of vision. So, periods of clouded vision, and periods of clear vision, have been my journey. Periods of despair, and then profound well-being. And out of that – it doesn't much matter which one I'm in – as long as I set aside "me," then I have something of value to share with people.

"Set aside me," as in put the sense of "me" aside.

Well, I think any athlete understands what I mean. There's a moment when you are trying to do what you're doing and you're awkward, you're clumsy, and then... You described Alia jumping off a steep hillside, and then leaping from rock to rock. And then you described yourself doing it. She was doing it without "me," and you were doing it with "me." The body is very awkward when there's "me," You know? You won't have a good tennis swing, you won't have a good golf swing, you won't ski smoothly, you know?

So, I mean literally, to do without doing. To live without guiding. To be undivided in what you do. That's to be without "me." Okay? When "me" is there, there is a spectator, a supervisor, a judge, an advisor, a critic. There's a strategy, a goal, a destination, there is a purpose when "me" is there. When "me" is not there, you're just doing it. You're just living it –

it's living you. You are breathing it, and – you are being breathed. You know, it's not my breath – it's breath. It's not my life – it's life. It's not my body – it's body. It's not my pain – it's pain. It's not my joy – it's joy. And that is what I mean by leaving the "me world."

The Dark Night Of The Soul

Let me ask about the Dark Night of the Soul. Specifically, as it has arisen as part of your own process and then perhaps beyond that, what your understanding is of that process in others, considering that you've had such an intimate awareness of so many people's spiritual journeys.

I often joke that, maybe my life would be different if it had been the white butterfly that landed on my forehead, instead of the black one. Form requires formlessness. Formlessness is terrifying to our egos, to our sense of personal identity. I truly believe that deeper consciousness is a continuous process of descending into the dark, which is that which is beyond our ability to understand and often seems threatening to us. And as we're being called toward a new consciousness, the ego perceives that as darkness. I mean, I would say that, if God got near us, and we were still in ego awareness, that would be terrifying, and our perception then of God would be as Demonic. If we weren't in ego awareness, and we were able to relax and just rest into being, and God got near us, it would be an honor, bliss, nirvana.

But, I think you don't stay there. People don't stay there and aren't meant to stay there because their next cycle would be to go back into the world and try to reorganize matters, so to speak, in a more coherent, more integral, integrated process. So the dark night for me was the loss of meaning, the loss of wanting to live, the loss of anything in life that seemed fulfilling. And it was hard to trust, very hard to trust, and there was an enormous amount of fear. The more my mind tried to understand what was happening, the more fear there was. I had to make my peace with not knowing. I would wake up each day and I would say, "Okay, if life gives me nothing but this, I will say "thank you." I'll be grateful." So for a while after the extraordinary period of wholeness there was a period of fear, nothing but this incredible raw vulnerability. And like St. John of the Cross, I came to call it the Dark Night of the Soul.

I don't think it's one thing. There's a kind of turning inward that's almost contrary to everything that life had been about, that I experienced. I felt that I had been brought to the experience of union, and then afterwards sort of cast down into darkness and had to find my way again, slowly. It's so far in my past now, yet when I talk about myself I say, "One hand reaches out beyond this world into another dimension, which we can call transcendence," so I sometimes just use the image of holding an angel. And the other hand reaches down into something so dark and disfigured, anguished and agonized that I call it almost demonic.

And I really believe that when people get too high, something tries to pull them down into the earth, into the body, which is what we often talk about when we mean demonic. And when people get too locked into the rigidity of ordinary life, then something comes to break that and lift us out of it. And so that the Dark Night of the Soul is a kind of descent into a kind of "no-man's land" until you develop the ability to be present in it. Once you can, you are operating a wholly new consciousness.

There's a Sumerian myth: it's a woman's myth called "The Myth of Innana" and it describes the descent of the outer or superficial woman to her dark, inner sister that awakens the goddess energy. It's in a very important myth for women, but for men as well. This myth is beautifully discussed in a book called *Descent to the Goddess* by Sylvia Brinton Perrera. It describes what it's like to be stripped of adornment, stripped of vanity, stripped of purpose, stripped of motivation, stripped of self-image and self-worth until there's nothing left but the function of awareness itself. And that's what I mean by the dark night, being stripped of all that formerly provided one with a sense of self until only awareness remains and it is an awareness that is no longer referent to "me."

And the more unconditional we are, the more non-reactive we are, the more quickly that descent happens, and then we're lifted back up. And so rather than seeing it as a constant cycling, from the one polarity to another, I see it as an enlarging sphere of consciousness, and the Dark Night of the Soul as the first truly major descent into unknown territory, and the loss of sense of self.

In my teaching, I say that the fundamental fear that we have as individuals, is of non-existence. And we fear the dark night, to whatever depth it's experienced, whether it is provoked because of loss of a loved one, loss of a child, serious illness, the approach of death, loss of career, or an experience like I have just been describing. The Dark Night is born of the soul's urge to go beyond its present dynamic, its present form in life, either in search of God, or to escape unbearable suffering. Whatever occasions the descent, we are presented with feelings we don't know what to do with, presented with thoughts that we don't know how to hold. We're presented with states of being through which we don't know how to see as a face of God. And, see as a benevolent face of God. They're terrifying faces, they're threatening faces.

So I believe that a human being's deepest work is to learn to hold these things, and that people who have descended deeply are the ones who help us hold it all. They're the ones who, when you're with them, offer permission to be with your fear, in a new way. And that is, to enter into what has been judged and reviled and rejected in the human experience. And to find in it something like God in disguise. In *Descent to the Goddess*, when Inana gets all the way down she meets her dark sister, the antithesis of her outer world consciousness. And it isn't until the reality of the dark sister is honored that Inana is allowed to come back to the surface, come back to ordinary consciousness, but changed forever. So that's a story of the Dark Night of the Soul. It existed prior to the dark night that St John of the Cross wrote about.

But the process of despair, which is another way that I speak about it, is a necessary part of life that is very difficult in our culture, because there is no permission for it. A person who is, let's say, really creative and goes through university and then takes a few years off to discover themselves in the world doesn't necessarily enter a dark night, but adolescence can be quite a difficult rite of passage. Then there are the people that I know who are retiring from work, or have succeeded in their work and are ready to leave it behind after many years of it. They're immediately thinking of their next project. I say to them, "Well, why don't you give your soul a time of emptiness, a time of not doing?" And for them, it's so threatening. They don't know who they are without a direction, a purpose and our culture advocates that, all the time. So less and less vacation time, more and more speed, more and more to do, less and less time. If you can't find the solace in ordinary life, if you can't find the Shakti in everyday activity, then you're still in "ascending" spirituality. So, when I was – unconsciously – in an ascending spirituality, I needed to be pulled down. Living anything that happens, just being with what Is, is the truest part of my life.

So we talked about it yesterday as desolation, consolation. But despair means literally to be without hope. Yet how can we face death, or fear, or suffering without hope? How can we let go of hope? What would that be like? What would it be like to say, "This state that I'm in now is just what it is. If I fight it, I will make myself incredibly unhappy." It's not unlike what I think you were saying when you quoted Master Charles: "When I try to understand – when I want to know what it's all about – that's when

The Dance Of Kundalini

I suffer." But some part of us always wants to know what it's all about, even though we can't. And so, most of the pearls of my life have come out of darkness. Most of who I am. And I've learned a certain mastery in darkness. A certain kind of keeping my own counsel and learning to be generous when I feel very vulnerable. So, standing very close to the light or the fire is also standing close to annihilation, not simply standing close to heaven. And then, in some periods, it resolves into *ahhhh* bliss. I don't see bliss as the goal; I see it almost as the relaxation that was brought about by the darkness – or the transparency that was brought about by the darkness. Transparency to me is, really, the heart of what happens. You know, you don't know who you really are. You don't know how much you're identified with your body, and how much you're identified with your thinking. You don't know how much you're identified with your world, your actions – until you feel like you're losing those things. And then, I mean, you knew Alia. You watched her being stripped of everything slowly but surely, and yet, she was still offering you a message.

The reason Alia was so close to me is because I've spent so much time in the darkness. And, I didn't have to tell her that. She knew it. Everybody that's been in the darkness knows it when they meet it in another. I often feel people who have been challenged in this way to be more real than the people who seem to know where they're going in life.

It's not a popular message. It's not one you can sell well. You'll find that if you read my books, or you listen to my talks, you'll meet it there. I'm basically always pointing people toward the fear that they don't want to face. And my life is about facing that *in my life*. Facing that in my marriage. Facing that in my work. Transparency is just that place where you are "in the world but not of the world," and you have to cling to your sense of identity, your sense of self, just enough to remain in the world. And yet you're being dissolved beyond the world and in that state between form and formlessness. I think there's a chapter about this in *The I That Is*

We called "Living at the Edge of Formlessness." I don't think I'm saying anything new. I think I've been saying the same things right along: that, you know, it hasn't been an easy life, yet it has been a remarkable life. And that's just how it is, whether it's my nature, or whether it's in my genes.

Franklin Merrell-Wolff, an American mystic philosopher whom I knew, felt at one point in his awakening process that he was going to leave the world, but that he was quite happy to do so. Then as he began to write, he started embodying himself. But he didn't suffer that process very much. We talked about that a little bit. It's always been important for me to talk about suffering because I meet so many people who suffer. Whether they suffer from illness or, more usually, from what their own minds create. I just called some people today because they'd called me last week and I spent an hour and a half or so on the phone with them – just to check in with a 44- year-old woman who has metastatic lung cancer. She never smoked in her life. It's in her brain now and she has grand mal seizures. And she's got two children, 14 years old and 10 years old, and she's going to die. She's got no spiritual foundation, no training whatsoever – none. And, she doesn't know how to meditate. Very few people can meditate at a time like this.

Can you imagine? They've not been given the tools to face suffering. What they want is hope. Medicine can provide no more hope and they've already gone through the ordeals of losing hair and chemotherapy, and yet they're still asking questions. What do I do? I say to them, "Listen. Be quiet and listen. You don't have to do something to save your life. You can let yourself die, and maybe you won't. If you keep listening, I think something will lead you. There's no promise it will be able to protect you from death." Some of them then say, "How do I listen?" And I say, "You have to get quiet and observe what it is that you're running from, or what it is that you're running to. Just take the running to, and put it aside for a while. And take the running from, and try to put that aside for a while also. And then listen."

I said to this woman, "What you really, really might want to do, is not do anything. And then you might just feel like *Ahhh, this seems like giving up*. And you could, in fact, be giving up. On the other hand, you could be opening up." It's just talking to that in people and knowing what a difficult place it is. What a difficult place it is for her husband. And as I was talking to them her 14-year-old son came in, so I could hear his voice for a minute and speak to him a little. So, I think what comes through me for that kind of person, is not answers, but somehow a space that makes it easier for them to be in the unknowing and the dark night of their lives. This is part of what I do. It's that part of what I'm journeying through.

I see a lot of people who are seeking to be free of it. And I'm saying, as Jesus said, "Those who seek to save their lives will lose it." It is one of the greatest paradoxes that the survival impulse in human beings is what's leading us to extinction. You have to not insist upon surviving in the face of annihilation. You must know when to lay yourself down in the darkness, in the abyss, lay yourself down with poise and dignity. If people say they feel like they've fallen into an abyss, I say, "Okay then, be sure to point your toes." Have you ever seen the people dive in Acapulco, off those 100-foot cliffs, into the ocean?

Yes.

What's the difference between someone falling off a diving board and a well executed dive? Well, the difference is, precision in the air, or form, and relationship to body and relationship to you who are in all of that. So if you're falling, and you're falling into an abyss, pointing your toes means keeping your eyes wide open, trying not to protect yourself from what you feel. Listening to what other people are saying. Fighting against the self-involvement that comes from fear – and is also the root of fear. So when self-involvement goes, fear goes too. Many people go through the dark night.

And it's not always the mystical dark night that leads to union with God, you know, but what's union with God anyway? That's just an idea, an idea that people talk about after they've had an experience they don't understand and which they've had nothing to do with. And unless that experience of union leads you to turn that into some new patterns in your life, it's hard to argue that it does much for us. Not much, that is, unless you really put your life into the *new* life. It is the injunction that new wine needs new wine skeins. I love how the old teachings keep coming back again and again.

Very beautiful. Thank you

The Second Fundamental Realisation – All Of Manifest Reality IS The Divine Mother

An area that I'd like to explore is the Divine feminine. You speak about a "second" realization in your book, The I That Is We. I understand it was something that happened while you were in India.

Yes, the second realization, the second fundamental realization. The first time it happened – when the black butterfly landed on me after the whole process that had started days before with this tremendous energy or Kundalini experience or whatever you want to call it – it was almost as if it came from outside. It was very much oriented to the Christ consciousness. Intuitively, I was seeking that consciousness, as a resolution to the state I was in.

But a year or so later, when I was at an ashram in India and I was doing this self-enquiry process, just sitting there working with the question, "Who are you?" and working with other people, I just suddenly felt this mounting sense of terror. It happened so fast: there was no explanation for why I should feel this way in the context that I was in; there was no threat to me. And I stayed, I didn't run away, I didn't try to go off and process it by myself. I just sat right where I was.

And suddenly I felt like my blood was literally turning to ice and I felt like I was exploding from the inside out. But then, just as suddenly, I felt that everything had become quiet and peaceful. And I realized ...not *felt as if*. This is so hard to describe – I call it: Existence Is the Mother. What it felt like was as if I was sitting on my mother's belly and I could feel her breathing, and I was going up and down with her breath, which was my breath. So, *I was being breathed*. But what was breathing me was existence. The totality, the sum totality of manifest reality as I could perceive or experience it in that moment; and it was my mother. It was as intimate to me and as nurturing of me as a mother is of an infant.

And I was like an infant. I was this undifferentiated consciousness. I was pure consciousness. And the womb that held me and consoled me and nurtured me and cared for me was existence. And that means in this context right now, everything you hear and perceive and sense – not a subtle world that's other, but *this* world, right here and now, but seen in a completely different way. And to me it was the Goddess, if you will – ah, that's a word I hung on it later. At the time, I called it Mother. I knew it wasn't my biological mother; there was no association to my physical mother. I didn't think in terms of Divine Mother, although when I tried to explain my experience later, I used those terms.

Instead of something that came from *without*, it felt to me like, and it made me feel like, I was one with everything. This was the feeling that everything was, in fact, nurturing me; everything in fact was the *womb*, in which I existed. It was just a very feminine, or female-oriented experience. There was no sense of thinking of it as transcendence or, God consciousness, or self-realization, or Christ consciousness. It was simply that existence is the Mother. I can't explain it. It's much less word-able to me than the first realization – and because I didn't have any background in praying to the Divine Mother or anything, I had no image for it. Certainly in Judeo-Christian religions, except in esoteric areas, they didn't until relatively recently have a strong feminine symbol.

I mean, they finally, in the "50s, elevated Jesus" mother to the pantheon of the Father, the Son, and the Holy Ghost. At last a female makes it to the big time. A major change in the collective unconscious, at least among Christians. My experience was just simply: this reality is the Divine Mother. This is her womb. It's all of it, not just nature. I mean, it's a big mistake when we equate the Divine Mother with nature. I think the Divine Mother is manifest reality. That includes everything human beings have manifested, even if, from another point of view, we think of some of it as pathological. In that state I didn't think about that. I didn't have a sense that there was something here that was sustaining me that shouldn't be here.

So I have never been able to speak of it easily, to make intellectual sense of it. But, I know that it complemented the first experience and it was almost nine months later, the second experience. Just as powerful as the first one. I think maybe it came to me because I was travelling the world by myself and I often felt alone. So maybe for that reason, to some extent, when this breakthrough occurred, it took the form of something profoundly nourishing and nurturing that felt like Mother.

Awakening In Relationship Is An Endless Process

There's the potential to kind of – to ask a question, that... There just isn't time... No, I'll just...

Trust yourself, completely.

(Laughs brightly)

Right now, I mean...Don't inhibit...I mean...The best thing that can happen is a relationship between us. Okay? So, if you're starting to get tranced out, don't get tranced out. Because if you go into a mode that's too receptive, you may lose contact with what you really want to say.

Yeah.

So, just go for it. And if you understand, or don't understand what I'm saying, or could say it in a way that's clearer – just say it!

Well, what I'm wondering now, and what you've spoken about – beautifully – are those aspects of the dissolution of the "me." You've gone into the way life functions in the absence of the "me"... This is taking the interview to perhaps a different level now – I'm asking about that process itself. Was there a point in your life that could be seen as a final integration, or was there a level of openness that arose, that made the oscillation a smooth and continuous circle?

Ahhh. Fair enough. "Is there hope?"

(Laughter builds... and bursts!)

"Is there hope... hope of... Is there resolution?" Yes, I would say, if I could isolate myself from the world, then this is integrated in me. There is now a much more smooth integration ... I used to frame it as *the ego as servant instead of sovereign*. But life is also ceaseless relationship. And there is no defined role for the Self. That is, if you choose a role that is an externalization of the Self, let's say as a master or as a guru, then you structure relationship in a way that people will defer to you. You experience the danger of becoming isolated. If you, in fact, realize that the Self is no-thing, and is therefore present even in your neurotic qualities, then in a certain sense you become transparent or invisible, and then any role you take on is like clothing you put on. Okay? And you can take it off. Which means that all relationships become relative. And all relationships have the right to challenge us, or to challenge "me." And all relationships are part of how I learn.

And so, when someone's suffering in a way that I'm not suffering, I don't just have advice for them – *they're my teacher*. I have to listen. If, in my marriage, I want to be seen the way that I like to be seen – doesn't everybody? – that's self-involvement. And if my wife points that out to me, and I react, then I have to deal with that kind of conflict. So of course, the oscillation between openness and contraction continues, but it is nowhere near as violent and painful as it used to be. It's much, much more integrated. The challenge comes in bringing whatever level of Self-realization we have touched into the world. Taking a larger consciousness and turning that into ordinary intimacy. Turning that into friendship. Turning that into healthy relationships. "Chopping wood and carrying water" in the field of daily necessity and ordinary relationships. Perhaps it's easier to take a solitary path, many spiritual teachers have done so. But whatever path we choose I believe there are consequences...both ways... positive and negative. So, I don't think one path is better than another, only they result in different expressions of consciousness. I don't know why I've chosen the path of relationship, and someone else might not. But, in answer to your question, I still cycle. But I understand it so well now, and I make room for it now. It hasn't become just smooth.

What does go unchanged is the silence…that is neither "me" nor "not me"… or the emptiness, that's neither "me" nor "not me." That never leaves me. That's always there. But what does that look like in a marriage? (Breathes a laugh.) What does that look like in a relationship with someone who sees you as just an employer, or sees you as a stranger seated next to you in an airplane? The easiest thing in my life is being a teacher. That's easy.

Vision – Inspiration – Expansion

Why do you say that being a teacher is easy?

Because I get out of my way. Because the level of relationship is proscribed and limited to a certain extent. Because it goes on for a few hours or a few days or a few weeks, and, while I have been in relationship with quite a number of people for many, many years, I'm not in relationship with them every day. Something happens in the crucible of intimate relationship that can't be escaped. You know, if you've had some real level of awakening or realization, but you don't have that piece in your bedroom, then you don't have that piece. And when I don't have it in my bedroom, I don't have it. I have questions about who I am; I have questions about my partner; I have questions about what is real or not real; I have questions about what is relationship; I have questions about "How does one live consciously?" without dictating to the other what "conscious living" should be like. How do… how do two… See, relationship isn't "me" … and it isn't "you" … It's a space between the two of us that holds us… that we create. Will it ever be fully smooth? Doesn't the creative process always have times of tension…does fertility also include infertility? Do you know what I mean? Doesn't creativity also have dry times? Doesn't the process of arriving at clarity also have times of deep obscuration? Of course!

In the world of necessity, the so called "daily grind," we each function as "me." And when you function as "me," you function in a constant cycling of various sub-personalities. And to realize who you are is to realize that which is unchanging, that views all these disparate parts of ourselves with equanimity. In the midst of that, therefore, one may be able to enter into the constant cycling of sub-personalities in new ways…ways that are more refined, more subtle, more complete…changing the patterns, as we were talking about at lunch, the patterns of behaviour.

I know there's a desire in people to have an endpoint, a resolution, a "happy ending." As we grow many things integrate, but if you look at nature, species now are going into extinction every day – and not just because of human action. They always have been. And new species are being created every day, though we may not recognize them right away. There are new species forming today. Maybe not at the same rate that they're going extinct. Certainly we cannot say there are new mammal species, no. But there are new bacterial species, and new viral species – we know that. Because AIDS is one of them, and so forth.

And so, there's a constant emergence of that which is new, and a constant dying off. And there isn't an endpoint to that. Nor do I think that there is any kind of endpoint to human consciousness, or how that can be expressed in our relationships, in how we structure our societies, and express our cultures. I think that our desire for an endpoint is a way that we fight against reality. I think it's hubris, a pride, that we have. So…there are times that I'm ashamed of some of the things that I feel, even still. And how long…how many times have I been aware – "Oh, you're feeling ashamed of your own feelings. You're feeling ashamed of your…of your anger. You're feeling ashamed of your doubt."

And, everywhere I go in the world, I see people are ashamed of what they feel. And… I just think that the people who have had deep realization are able to see these things, the judgments, the shame, as objects – psychological objects. So for them, it's not that they don't feel them; it's that they're not so identified with them. But…if I'm not identified with something, yet continue to manifest it, to let it influence my behaviour, and that behaviour disturbs my wife, that's a struggle. However, if I'm not identified and she too can look at some behaviour in me and say, "Oh, I know that about you. And I know you're more than that," then we've made space for our personalities and the relationship thrives. If she has something in her that she's unhappy about, and I criticize her for it or judge her, that's pain for her. That's misery. If she has that in her, and I can forgive it, then there's space in her to forgive it as well. When two or more are gathered, together, we create the real…the actual consciousness.

It's important, then, to say that awakening is a stage, but awakening in relationship to one's infinite depths and all the other possibilities of human relationships is an endless process! There's a realization of self, and then there's a realization of self in a marriage, which is endless. Or a realization of self in a community which is endless. And the realization of self in a community is why we now have more relationships that follow the principle of democracy. That's why there's more suffrage for women, and more and more liberty for people to own property, things that just weren't available before.

So, I feel like my struggle for consciousness is part of the birth struggle everywhere. To me, whether it's when we're moving in a direction that is, let's say, rising to a higher vibration in meditation – leaving behind "me" – a kind of disincarnating movement – then we enter into joy and bliss; there is a cessation of struggle. But the minute we take that energy and we want to bring it down into a more subtle, more differentiated way of relating, in a family or in a community then we are incarnating that consciousness and this is invariably stressful at first.

I just put this out for you, (Richard produces a large print on cloth of the Earth as seen from space). I travel with this, I use this image as a kind of mandala, at the centre of a circle of people, to open us to a particular kind of discussion. This is what they call an "Earth Flag." And you had asked me about the Earth, and at some point we can get into a conversation about that...

But just to finish the thought that I'm in, which is just simply, that the incarnating process – taking Spirit and bringing it into the world – is hard. We have to see our old patterns and work to change our thinking, our beliefs, our behaviour. It would be a lie for me to say that I don't struggle to live more fully the things that I teach. It was in some sense easier when I had a community of people around me that were in service to my work as was the case years ago. I didn't have to cook and I didn't have to clean, and I didn't have to go shopping; I could sit and embody the transformational energy, to sit in that higher presence and radiate it. But I chose to leave that – so now, I cook and I clean and I go shopping, and I coordinate our home improvements with contractors and gardeners, and I have for many years. In my present life I have access to that higher energy, but I am living in a much more ordinary role, where it is much easier to slip into the basic patterns from much earlier in my life. So my life is more cluttered now, but more like everybody else's life, or most people's life. I think spiritual teachers can create a context in which people just come and listen to them and where the teacher is constantly fed by the student's attention. And certainly, India is a culture that honors that context of relationship – I was once, years ago, invited to create an ashram in India.

Oh?

When I was travelling through India in the late '70s and early '80s and people would sit next to me and feel the energy they'd say, "Would you create an ashram here, and teach us?" And I'd just look at them and think to myself, "Boy, that would be neat," but I would never do it, because I knew they were sensing just one element of my being, and that there was a lot more I needed to do to integrate the more neurotic and fearful parts of myself.

I think I'm trying to answer your question in two different levels. If I identify with the struggle, then I'm struggling. If I see that the struggle is intrinsic to creativity, then, I don't struggle very much. If you, for example, when you were talking about how challenging this book is – the kinds of emotions this book is taking you into – see the struggle as inherent to the creative process then you don't need to judge yourself negatively as part of you has been. You are trying to give birth to something you don't yet know how to hold fully. If you're giving birth to something and you're not sure what it is, then you're not sure you're giving birth to something healthy or not. You're not sure whether you're giving birth to that which is just self-serving, just another game of your ego. If you're not even sure you know how to do it, but you're working to do it – that creative process is hard, and there is suffering in it, and I think that suffering can be minimized by understanding that the creative process is hard and by finding the rhythm of determination, commitment and surrender to the process. What I hear myself talking about is not only you writing a book, or me writing a book, or me unfolding my work as a teacher; I see it as human society, human cultures, building sustainable economies and environmentally friendly forms of business. And, I see this as happening everywhere. I know how easy it is to stay in the pattern that we know, even if it's leading to annihilation. And how hard it is to change a pattern for an unknown pattern.

So, to have this kind of a conversation serve as a spiritual teaching; it really doesn't serve people to just sit around me and listen to me. It serves them to listen to me for a while and then go out into the world and find out what it's like to bring more integrity and authenticity into their relationships, and then come back and have another conversation. That's the form my work takes.

I understand that about you, that people come; gather for a while, and people often do that with a spiritual context from what I can see. Even if there's an ashram set up and there's a group of dedicated disciples, those disciples are serving a space that other people visit for a while on retreat.

Yeah, I mean it in that way, but, I also mean it in a slightly different way. People should dip into special places – retreats – spend time with someone who inspires and challenges them, and then return to their life. They should, but it's also how they return to their life, what the emphasis is, that's important. For example, if you meet the people that have spent time with me over the years, you'll discover that they're free to be Buddhists or they're free to continue with, or follow Gnostic Christianity, or Judaism or whatever. Or they're free to be non-religious but deeply spiritual in their own ways. They tend not to be elitists; they tend not to be exclusive; they tend not to create communities of identity around so-called spiritual teachings. What they tend to do is go out and create meaningful relationships in their communities. And a community is, as soon as there are two people gathered together, two or more – that's a community.

I think that that's a very important thing that people have observed about my work over the years, or what has magnetized around me, is that it's not exclusive, it's not elitist, there's no identification with me as the teacher or the community as a special group. I'm important, but I'm not at the centre of it. I am at the centre of it only in brief periods when I'm focussing as a particular piece of work. But I'm only at the centre of it as an instrument for something else, which is much larger than me, much larger than my ideas about consciousness and much more important than this brief life of mine. And I have to re-energize myself, regularly. I have to re-motivate myself, regularly. I have to find the love for the people I'm going to spend time with, people I may be meeting for the first time, over and over again, in service to that larger vision. And if the vision is just about me and how I want to spread a particular teaching in the world, then that's not a pleasant state for me. It's only helpful when I can get out of my way and become a servant once again.

So there's being a servant, and at the same time wanting to pay my bills by charging people money to receive whatever you want to call this – I would call it in this instant "soul nourishment." It's about vision, authenticity, inspiration, the enlarging of consciousness. It's about understanding one's own mind and practicing self-inquiry. I teach people the power of their awareness through our work and then ask them to go home and practice it. What I share is that the way we live ordinary life, is the spiritual practice. Okay, so that's what I do. I try to teach people how to learn; how to learn to see themselves without judgment; how to stand outside of their patterns. How to act in the present moment in a way that changes the old patterns, without any assurance that it's going to lead to a desired outcome. In this sense the work of growth and change is really a movement in faith, an activity that is, in itself, faith. You are not just inserting some kind of spiritual practice into your life to achieve enlightenment or liberation. You cannot know what the outcome will be. It is your life. The outcome is your life, right now.

I am defining spiritual work as anything that increases our capacity for healthy relationships. It is about the marriages we build, how we raise our children, the communities we create. And that all starts from where we each start from within ourselves. For me the goal is not some kind of spiritual realization, some kind of satori, or samadhi, some experience that is imagined to be an end in itself. I kind of laugh at the idea of seeking enlightenment in that conception. What happened to me when I woke up

I actually had nothing to do with. I haven't met anybody who had anything to do with whatever woke them up. Even if it happens in the context of a spiritual retreat, the experience always transcends the context in which it occurred. Did you have anything to do with what happened to you?

No.

Not really. So you can't claim it. You can say, "I can report this happened, and I'm probably not reporting it properly or accurately," but you can't say, "It's mine! I'm enlightened!" You can't say that because you didn't do it. So enlightenment is the one thing that we can be absolutely sure none of us can claim.

Aha!

Therefore, it becomes meaningless to do a practice in order to lead to enlightenment. Meaningless to me, anyway. It's ass backwards. It's the wrong way around. Rather, it's do a practice so that you can learn to have a new relationship to yourself in the moment, and then see what you have learned in the mirror of your relationships. If the relationships go sour because people aren't as enlightened as you are, then you haven't learned very much at all.

Man And Woman, The One That Has Become Two

You mention that you feel that the realization that's coming forth collectively in this period of human evolution is the realization of the Divine Feminine. I've heard you say that several times. What's your sense of that?

Well, we can appreciate historically the devaluation and discounting, in many ways, of women. We see a strong polarization between men's and women's roles, and circumstances where women have been for a long time and in some parts of the world still remain essentially the property of men. In some cultures women can be killed or executed for adultery, where a man wouldn't be. In India among certain groups women are still expected to kill themselves when their husbands die. We see what appears to be a significant imbalance in most societies between the rights of women versus those accorded to men. I believe that as long as this imbalance remains unconscious it negatively influences our capacity for mutually empowering relationships. The effect is that we do not realize our deeper masculine nor feminine potential and this has profound effects throughout every arena of human activity.

I think that it's the task of men and women who are seeking to grow in consciousness to challenge that imbalance and try to find a new appreciation and respect for each other. We need new eyes for seeing each other and new ears for listening to each other. We need to assume that our perception of each other is skewed, that we have been blinded and deafened to each other's essence by our enculturation. We need to try to deconstruct our cultural biases, in particular penetrate into the subtle nature of male entitlement, and the limitations we assume about a woman's place in the world. As men we have to start to let the goddess energy live in our women even if it scares us, even if it threatens us. Part of the task now is to make up for the insidious disturbance in women's psyches that has come about through the way they have been treated and seen and mirrored by patriarchal societies. This is not only essential for women, but it is equally vital for men as well, because until the goddess energy has more fullness in women's lives, men remain emotionally and spiritually undeveloped as well.

We can't simply blame men or patriarchy because that doesn't actually teach us to listen deeply into who we really are, into how the One consciousness is expressed so uniquely in woman as compared to man.

And so, it's this restoration to a woman of something that has been distorted by the patriarchal forces. But just as a man can't become fully a man without something that a woman brings to him, so too a woman can't become fully a woman without something that a man brings to her. It is a transformation we must co-create together. An empowered woman, however that might look, means that any man in relationship to that woman will also be empowered. Said in another way, the full potential of man or woman resides in something that emerges through their relationship of each to the other.

Just to be inclusive, I understand that there's a certain percentage of the population who are homosexual. But even in homosexual relationships there is a division of masculine and feminine consciousness within the relationship between two men, or between two women. I believe even in these situations the general consciousness of men and women is also expressing itself whether the relationship is hetero or homosexual.

There's a way that a man mirrors the divine feminine in a woman and starts to acknowledge it and in so doing is himself transformed. You start to empower the goddess and She empowers you. You start to be a servant of that, as a man. And not expect the woman to be your servant in all the unconscious ways emotionally undeveloped men expect women to be. You stop expecting the woman to be your mother, to fulfil your every need, to be your lover, your foil, your concubine, and in so many ways carry your emotional life for you. You start to see her as divinely inspired, as goddess. Now, these are words, but the process is a profound communion that takes place energetically and is usually undermined by the superficial level in which we argue and talk about our differences, and our uniquely felt needs. When we try to talk about who we are as men and women we usually end up polarized and caught in the same old assumptions and conditioning.

To live this process, first the energy must be actualized and then perhaps the attempt to put what is happening into words can follow. To actualize this energy we have to go beyond reacting to the anger and fear our apparent differences tend to generate, and especially our culturally conditioned expectations of each other. We have to learn to merge our energy fields and then remain in deep presence together as that larger energy begins to awaken us to deeper levels of ourselves.

A man usually sees "his woman" as an object – a sex object, or a comforter. He sees a woman as an inspiratrix, maybe someone to help him in his creative expression, you know. He sees her as a mother to carry and protect his emotional life, to explain him to himself emotionally. He sees her as the mother of his children; he sees woman as mother in that form. But, where do men see woman as wisdom? Woman as divinely inspired, as a manifestation of a transcendental intelligence that we must listen to? Especially when we think we, as men, are seeing clearly and we don't really grasp the subtlety of a woman's way of sensing into situations and how she sees in a way unique to woman. We implicitly see her perception and way of processing information and experience as inferior. It has been conditioned into us to believe this. Even women have believed it. How do we listen to her, and help her listen to that transcendental intelligence that only she, as a woman, can tune into? Because we, as men, can't tune in the same way, because we're men. That's what I said to you in the restaurant – that human beings are not men, or women. A human being is a man and a woman. The one has to become two.

So this true consciousness, that is, the consciousness of the human being, needs the man and the woman to be discovered, to be evoked, to be brought forth and followed, and manifested. And we have not given enough room to the woman as the carrier. She's not the other half, or "the better half," of a discrete unit of intelligence; she and he are two infinities of intelligence that together create something that's more than either, and transcends either.

Think about this image of a man who's going to unconsciously obey the patriarchal mentality and assume certain rights and privileges for himself that he does not recognize for a woman. He may believe he has the right to dominate her. He will project onto her the things I just listed – lover, mother, mother of children, emotional enigma, carrier of the psychological and emotional. Likewise, you see the woman projecting onto the man: he's the spiritual one, the mystic, the "rock," the problem solver; she is always trying to understand and explain his psychology at the expense of looking at herself. Her man is also the "father" figure, the meaning giver, even if that meaning comes in reaction to his behaviour, his betrayals, his needs at the expense of recognizing her own. Or he is the "lover," the bringer of passion and safety, and thus also the one who can take away security, meaning and love. So she seduces him, tries to control him, and she believes she needs him to be complete. She does not have a true sense of self in which the goddess energy in her, the divine intelligence in her, is being called forth. So when you have a man who is caught in the patriarchal mind set, he tends to attract and be attracted to a woman who hasn't got a strong sense of self, because he hasn't got an authentic sense of self either.

We look out at the world and we see literally billions of men living with billions of women. We see the nexus right there of the future, because each couple is going to pass on the cultural values, nurture, and socialise their children in accordance with their level of self-realization. And if the goddess energy is only allowed to be expressed in that couple through only a few of its channels, such as mothering, what do the children then inherit psychologically?

All men are born of woman. So how do so many men learn so little respect for women? All women are born of woman, so how do so many women have so little respect for being woman? The ordinary man is terrified of the goddess energy in a woman and as long as he tries to suppress her or overcome her with physical punishment or the domination of social rules or religious precepts he will remain a very small person.

And women are afraid of their goddess energy, because the "little girl" in each woman is afraid of being abandoned and not loved. So to be loved becomes equivalent with not shining her divine light. As women are waking up, they have the power to express that light. She has the power to turn that light on the man in her life and show him his self-involvement and his self protection and his patriarchal sense of entitlement which is really a mask for his fear of the goddess, and the convenience (for avoiding deep relationship) of his self-importance. If she can wake him up to this unconscious smallness in him, without destroying him, without him withdrawing and closing down, then something can be born between the two of them that never existed before in either. The divine feminine cannot live without its escort in the divine masculine and vice versa.

I think this emergence of the goddess energy simultaneously with a new male consciousness is happening very inclemently in the collective consciousness, but it's happening in certain couples, here and there. And it's happening because relationship is so essential to us and it's failing everywhere. Sixty-eight percent of second marriages end in divorce within five years. Over fifty percent now of first marriages end in divorce in the same time period. That's gigantic suffering. In the modern world, at least in my experience as I travel and teach, relationship stress is the most prominent form of suffering. And where there is suffering and we begin to turn the light of inquiry toward ourselves we grow spiritually. To grow spiritually doesn't mean we look for religion to answer our questions to define men's and women's roles according to scripture. Religion in this sense is an argument for the status quo; it cannot give us spiritual growth. Spiritual growth is literally new behavior and potentials that are emerging from spirit. It is the emergence of unrealized potentials; it is the birth of something new out of the alchemy of suffering and the inquiry that leads to.

To me this is the fundamental work for our time. And in my marriage, we are struggling to live this. It can be very hard work at times, and it's slow. It's not – plug in this formula for a loving marriage and here's how it works. It's not – we romanticize the marriage, and we eroticize how to have "hot sex." For me, it's really how to start changing the pattern of how I reflect her to herself, and how I hold her in myself. And that's regardless of what she does for me, or to me, or how she sees me. It's hard work and its easy to think at times, "Well, maybe we're not right for each other." but that's what everybody thinks when there is pain and confusion and we believe that our suffering is a sign that something is wrong. But a large reason why it seems wrong is that we are not doing real work with each other. We are still looking to romantic images of how we imagine a relationship should be and not really listening to what we are each doing in ourselves and between each other. I think we're only right for each other if we mirror that which is right in the other.

Sex is so important to a relationship because the first thing that withers in a relationship when it's not working is sex. When intimacy isn't happening, when the communication isn't happening, libido goes. Even a relatively young man can wonder if he is impotent. But in a long-term relationship there are so many intrusions by all the necessities of daily life. Combine that with people who are not sitting in their energetic core, then the male-female polarity is lost. There is a male body and a female body living together, but the minds are far, far away from the bodies, caught in fear of abandonment, judgement, disillusionment, unmet needs. When the mind and the body are not united, there is no energetic polarity and sex weakens. To restore that polarity we have to get reconnected with our essential energy and start to merge with each other's energy fields.

But conditioned roles and expectations eventually cut both the man and the woman off from that. So the relationship begins to fail and there is suffering. It is a wake-up call. Sexual attraction is temporary. For a deeper attraction to live the man and the woman have to help each other find their way back to something essential. Each has to help the other realize God. Wow! Because the vast majority of people, and I think this is more true of men, unconsciously seek realization and spiritual experience so they can be immunized from the challenge of relationships, so they can transcend stress, so they can sort of sit on a cloud some place and be above the fray. It's really escape from suffering that they're looking for, not embodying God, which frankly I do not think is possible without deeply discovering the full potential of male/female relationships.

Creativity And The Intelligence Of The Body

Could we speak about creative activity? I get a sense that creativity may be part of an integrative process for you.

Well, creativity is many things. When I spend a lot of time writing, then that needs to be balanced with being more fully in my body: walking or going to the gym to exercise or swim. I love to do things with my hands. I used to do a lot of sculpting in hard dolomite or soft marble. Nowadays, there's no end of things to do here with the orchards. All of it is creative to me, but I think of creativity as being in balance, so that the mind rests naturally back into stillness.

The awakening process gives us new energy. That energy needs to be used or it becomes stagnant, morbid. And it needs to be used in new ways.

If you think about Zen, for example, in a Zen community and Zen tradition as a person undoes the old, they have to create some way of expressing the new. They can do that in martial arts, they can do that in drawing, they can do that in art, or in service work. So to me, creativity is not art, per se, but the process by which that which is unfolding from within oneself has a way to find form. And whatever the form is, it needs to balance the new energy. Because if you have energy that's been awakened and you don't use it, it becomes morbid. So you need to use it.

Lately, as I have been working on my new book, I regularly reach a point when my thinking isn't working well, or I'm not really flowing, so then it's time to step outside and take up the chisel. The particular piece that has been accompanying me through this recent writing process, I have been working on for about three years. Holding the chisel, tapping it gently, visualizing what needs to be removed and what will remain, letting the whole project evolve as the rock allows it, is all a wonderful change of focus from writing that brings me back into balance.

I don't see myself as a writer or a sculptor. I write when the urge is strong as a balance to the insight and energy that has grown in me over the previous years as I was teaching. I sculpt for the same reason, as enjoyable in itself and as a balance to whatever else I am doing. My last book was *The Second Miracle,* in the mid 90s, and now this book, which is entitled *The Mandala of Being,* that I'm currently writing has been a long time in gestation. In my earlier life, before Ariel and I made a family together, when I lived much more contemplatively, monastically, in about a period of seven years I wrote three books. And in the eighteen years since then, I've written only one more. Just because my life has been so full with other things, in addition to teaching.

But, for instance, each time I give a talk is a creative process. I don't make notes and I don't give the same talk twice. Each time I sense into what wants to speak *through me*. I attune to the audience and out of that listening let the process of giving a talk emerge. In my work, I invite a lot of body-centred activity – as you may remember. It can be dancing, or breathing, or whirling. I use whatever frees us to experience the body as a matrix for present moment consciousness, as opposed to using or directing the body to perform in a certain way, or look a certain way. Letting oneself be danced instead of guiding the dancing is how I understand a body-centered creativity.

So it is, in large measure, engaging the body?

Yes. Because to my way of thinking, the body is the most intelligent part of us. The next most intelligent is the feeling nature, and then the least intelligent part of us is the intellect, the way that we interpret information, create beliefs and evaluate ourselves and our world. It is important to differentiate intellect from awareness. The "awareness" capacity in us is not intellect. It's Consciousness itself. But that Consciousness, when we experience it in its fullness, is very much a bodily experience, a bodily experience of presence, a bodily experience of bliss and wonder. So if you want to be led out of your intellect, which lives in the past, in the future, and in psychological constructions that we call me, and constructions about other people, then the body is the best way, because it is always in the present. That's why I work with the body.

I've always personally enjoyed physical activity: hiking, dancing, rock climbing, swimming, skiing. Right now I've been struggling with a little bit of a back problem – some sciatica problem – and an old shoulder injury that I re-injured in yoga class. But ordinarily I love to climb and hike, and today I was out for a jog with the dogs. I just enjoy those things and do them because I become so absorbed in nature and the immediacy of the moment. And in my work it long ago became clear that if we want to expand in consciousness we also have to be more in our bodies, more in the now. Intellectual knowledge can be acquired by studying and gathering information and this serves us in certain narrow contexts. But deeper knowledge comes through the whole being. There is no spirituality without the body.

When The Earth Says No

One thing in your relationship to life, as I perceive it, that really moves me is your relationship with the Earth, and the depth of feeling and importance that you obviously give to this topic. So what would you like to say about our relationship with Mother Earth?

Well, simply – I just said that the body is the most intelligent dimension of our being, and I think that in people who are truly wise, their intelligence flows from their bodies, you sense it as a radiance, a presence. But this planet is what our bodies emerge from. And so, the wisest people have always learned by observing nature and seeing their own intelligence reflected in Her. Planet Earth is the sum of an incalculably complex system of relationships from subatomic dynamics, to chemical processes, to the incredible dance of life in all its forms.

I believe what we call Earth is actually a consciousness that is the sum total of all the forms of consciousness we observe on the Earth and that human consciousness draws its fullest potential in resonance with the consciousness of the planet and every individual consciousness on it. The Earth is much more complex than any corporation, any institution, or any nation or government, or the emerging global economy. Throughout time, we human beings have taken form in the fertile richness of the Earth.

Nowadays, we have forgotten our origins in the Earth. We move less and less in nature; we control nature, we dominate nature. It's dark outside right now as we talk, but it's light in here. It's cool outside but it's warm in here, and so on. We begin to forget the need of cycles: we forget that there's winter, we forget that there's spring, we forget that there's a time for quietness and incubation and hibernation, and a time for flourishing and extravagance and the burgeoning of buds and fragrances.

We have lost an earthly starting point in which to hold up a mirror to ourselves. In regard to this disconnect, we can ask ourselves a question: Is it possible to know if our thinking is healthy or not? Because suppose you like some ideas, or favour some beliefs or values, but you don't personally like or accept others? Perhaps your father believes one way, but your teacher another. Or your religion tells you one thing, but another religion says something else. How do you know which is right, or best, or healthiest? How do you know if your ideas about reality are consistent with reality or not?

The answer to this, I believe that the Earth can and is telling us those answers all the time. In the last analysis, it is the Earth that ultimately says *"no"* to human ideas, or *"yes."*

You're saying that the most intelligent part of us is the Earth?

Yes. That's what I'm saying. The Earth. It says, *"No, this doesn't work for you or Yes this does!"* Simple as ABC. If the Earth says *yes* – we thrive. If the Earth says *no* ... we get sick. If we grow too much food without replenishing the soil we gradually lose food production capacity. If we let our population grow too fast and we use chemicals to grow our food, those chemicals begin to poison us. If we use energy in a way that causes the planet to grow too warm our cities may eventually flood, cattle will die, plants and animals will go extinct and we will suffer and many of us will die. It's a simple, elegant and intelligent feedback to us. Unfortunately, it seems that our response to this feedback is not very intelligent. So the Earth will keep answering us until we get the message.

At this most extraordinary time – perhaps for the first time in human history, as far as any of us know, except perhaps for the mythic story of Atlantis – the Earth is starting to say *no*.

We know that nomadic tribes lived off the earth, and that when the game was decreased in an area, they just picked up and went somewhere else. They left a pretty big mess behind them. Not a horrible mess, not like we do – not toxic chemicals, and certainly not a bad mess, but a mess. However, it was a mess the Earth could heal.

If you step into an archaeological dig, or, or you go to parts of the foothill mountains of the Sierras here, as I have, and you see where the Native Americans have lived, you'll notice that where the soil is, it's oily, for a foot deep. That's because of all the animals they killed and the fat that seeped into the soil, and things like that. They polluted, but not with the kinds of chemicals we pollute with, and their impact was miniscule compared to what is happening now. So our ancestors were nomads and they migrated to find what they needed. But now there's no place to go.

In the summer of 1969, when Neil Armstrong stepped for the first time on the moon, and turned his camera back toward the Earth we suddenly had a picture of whole planet floating in the vast void of space. For the first time we had a symbol for who we really are: Earthlings. It is a symbol that doesn't show any national boundaries, that shows one wholeness. Since then we have learned that human activity is impacting the climate in dangerous ways. Most intelligent people now accept this to be true. We can think of this as the Earth saying, "What you're doing isn't good for you, because I can't protect you from yourselves. I can only mirror what you're doing that isn't good for you." And that's why the Earth is so important. We are so conflicted in our ideas, beliefs and values that we do not know how to say "No" to ourselves. The Earth is doing it for us.

And so, I think, for me, it's not just my love of the Earth that inspires me to do my retreats in places where nature is very present and accessible. It's also because nature mirrors the deep movement in people which you'd not see in a hotel room. If you really want to find silence and vastness, and generosity and gratitude and the rightness of all things, and interconnectedness, you don't want to do that in a classroom or a hotel conference room! For me, I don't find it in churches, even the magnificent ones in Europe. For me and for my work, I choose places where people can rest under a tree, or meditate on a rock, put their feet into a stream, watch birds flying, hear the wind, see snakes, hear coyotes, watch the moon and stars at night, and be alone in nature. You know how many people don't know what a really starry night is? Because they live in cities. I was raised in the suburbs of New York City; I went to school in the suburbs, in the yet somewhat rural areas that are now chock-a-block with development. Then I went to medical school in the heart of Manhattan and more training in the San Francisco Bay Area. I became a city person for a while. But later in life when I discovered the mountains and the deserts, the true miracle of this planet began to live in me. Eventually, I moved to the high dessert at the edge of a great mountain range. I saw mountain lions and so much other wildlife. I slept out many nights and watched the Milky Way circling in the night sky. For eight years we lived off the grid and in that wonderful setting I did my work and witnessed the power of nature to support our awakening.

It will sound strange that for all my sorrow at what I see happening to our environment, it also makes me happy. Life is finally announcing to our human egos, "What you are doing isn't working!" We may not listen and we will suffer. The Earth as we know it, whole landscapes and many forms of life, will be gone forever. But the opportunity to come into alignment with the intelligence of the Earth has never been as present to us as it is now. The possibility and the depth of change in human consciousness is awesome to contemplate.

I consider some of the natural disasters to be rather big slaps for humanity.

Hopefully we will let ourselves be humbled. But in our defense, we can only know that what we are doing is not sustainable because of the destruction we cause – we couldn't know it beforehand in a system as vast and complex as our planet. So if we destabilize the environment, that's going to be what's necessary for us to understand more about how the complex relationships that comprise this planet work. And that understanding will require us to limit our self-interest until our interests and the Earth's best interests are in accord.

We are approaching a collective Dark Night of the Soul. Our beliefs about religion, nationality, economics, and many other things are leading us to a crisis of values and identity as nations and even more so as a species. We don't need to blame ourselves for what we could not understand until now. But we now need the courage to make a profound change. I have watched many people learn they have a terminal illness and then make profound changes in their way of living. Well it is possible that we collectively have a terminal illness. We suffer from terminal pride in our intelligence not recognizing that we call intelligence is actually often intellectual arrogance and ignorance. The Earth by presenting us with a non-negotiable "No" is giving us a chance to reassemble our lives, to choose different values, with a different sense of purpose, with different limits, because as we watch extinctions and more powerful storms and see what we are losing, we can begin to learn what really matters to us.

And what really matters is relationship. What really matters is listening. What really matters is being present for each other. That's what really matters. And what really matters with the Earth is, now that we've learned how to mess it up, let's stop messing it up. Maybe we can actually do better. Maybe our consciousness can join with the Earth to actually create enhanced environments. I believe that's possible. That would be intelligent.

Enhanced — so that we're actually giving back to the Earth? Making it easier for the Earth?

Yes, why should human consciousness only create entropy and degradation? Why could it not also create greater coherence? Greater consciousness! Yes, why not? I mean, we ourselves, move from lower to higher states of consciousness, organically and naturally. So why couldn't Earth's ecosystems become even more sublime, even more complex, even more enriched if we were to join our consciousness with it more completely?

Why couldn't our love, why couldn't our attention, why couldn't our technologies be a form of worship consecrated to creating environments in which all things thrive, and through which we could even restore the environment? The evidence shows that prayer restores people to health, though no one knows how this happens. It suggests that consciousness is a broad field that contains and responds to each of us. I believe it contains all of the Earth and beyond the Earth. Why couldn't our way of treating the Earth be a prayer that restores health to the planet, that revitalizes ecosystems? Maybe it's science fiction — spiritual sci-fi. But my work has shown me the power of a small group of people to empower every individual within that group. Right now human consciousness is very fragmented and too many of us are the victims of fear in so many forms. That fragmentation of our consciousness weakens us and makes us susceptible to our worst tendencies. But when enough of us realize that the Earth is speaking to us, mirroring our present consciousness back to us, saying "NO," we will have for the first time in human history a call to unity that does not have at its foundation some ideology, some controversial belief system. We will have the concrete, unassailable reality of this planet on which we will either thrive or sicken and die.

So I encourage people to contemplate the photograph of the Earth from the moon and to have this conversation on the last morning (speaking of his retreats) because I want us to think about this. I want us to think about how good it is that the Earth is saying no. Instead of being afraid they can feel really good that the Earth is saying no. So many people are afraid about what's happening with the environment, and I keep on saying, "Don't be afraid; it's what we had to see before we could understand."

David Spero

Introduction
Liberation Through Kali's Fierce Grace

This was to be my first meeting with David Spero. Until this point we had spoken on the telephone and corresponded via e-mail. I was moved to include David's unique story in this book after reading his own account of a powerful spiritual awakening in his book *Beyond the place of laughter and tears in the land of devotion,* which I found to be lucid, insightful, and deeply inspiring.

After undergoing a series of profound spiritual awakenings, he found himself living spontaneously in full awareness of pure nondual consciousness, within which the fathomless energy of Shakti radiated endlessly in an ecstatic mystical condition of cosmic embrace. Remarkably, while in this highly evolved yogic state David suddenly found his nervous system being invaded by an intensely active feminine presence, a presence David refers to as Kali or simply the Mother. This deity-like manifestation usurped the functioning of his psychosomatic apparatus so completely as to obliterate the divine condition of cosmic oneness that he was living in. In a wild, unimaginable, and devastating encounter, David's nervous system was inundated completely by this cosmic presence, which systematically crushed every concept and state within him, including all spiritual states. Taking him *through* and finally *beyond* all states of consciousness and meditative awakenings, into the very source from which all awakening springs, finally leaving him *demolished* in a stateless state he refers to as spontaneous *functioning* and *primordial innocence.*

After a colourful bus ride from the California coast into the desert, I arrived in Palm Springs to be picked up from the bus station by Orley, David Spero's partner. A retired professor of law, Orley is a gentle man with a convivial nature, sporting a wry grin and a compassionate twinkle in his eye. He struck me as someone who possesses a kind of natural human wisdom. A little worn out by the bus trip and in need of a shower, I was whisked away in a sporty white Toyota Matrix past the flashy trimmings of the city and into the palm-studded suburbs, where cosy homes and gardens are surrounded by tall rocky mountains and blanketed by the most amazing sapphire blue sky.

As fortune would have it, I arrive just in time to partake of a talk David is giving at his home this weekend. I enter David's home to find there is nothing in particular to distinguish this as the home of a young Spiritual Master, except perhaps the brass statue of the Divine Mother who is depicted crushing an unsuspecting Shiva underfoot whilst stabbing him in the chest with her spear – an image very fitting to David's unique spiritual journey.

David Spero is something of a spiritual enigma. Possessing a clear, sparkling, and deeply insightful mind, he also displays a childlike spontaneity and innocence. The defining feature of David's life prior to his awakening was his absolute devotion to the task of penetrating into the very heart of the Divine Reality. Possessing no desire to succeed in worldly undertakings, David gave himself wholeheartedly to a life of meditation and spiritual inquiry.

The "enlightenment gathering" (David's term for satsang) that day was filled with penetrating insight, humour, and a luminous energy. Taking the form of a casual gathering of friends in a warm and friendly atmosphere, the whole event had a relaxed quality to it, the kind that made me think of it as being akin to a kind of Taoist spiritual party. A feeling of deep permission to *BE* filled the room, this unmistakable *sense of ease* in the atmosphere, I would soon learn, literally floods the vicinity around David.

My first impression of David was that of his total lack of pretense, his freedom from self-protective reservations and barriers. His moods and spontaneous expressions of feeling had a childlike quality to them. Interviewing David was an absolute joy, to say the least, and I might add, something of a roller coaster ride. He didn't appear to exhibit any set pattern of behaviour or fixed way of being. One moment he would be absolutely self-effacing, declaring himself to be nothing, a nobody, just functioning naturally and spontaneously "like a hummingbird," as he likes to say, and in the very next breath he spoke from the viewpoint of the Godhead, taking claim for the functioning of the whole universe. While I am no stranger to the paradox of intuitive spiritual understanding, there was something in the sheer force of conviction from which David spoke that brought the subtle philosophical nuances of nonduality squarely in front of me with such a profound living quality that they simply could not be ignored.

These types of juxtapositions, presented in such innocent self-abandon, caused my head to spin, as I found my mind could form no solid image of David, to which I could point and say "Ah yes, he is like this." Along with this, my own internal world was constantly shifting in response to David's chameleon-like ways. One moment I would be in shock, then confused, then suddenly I would be filled with the deepest feeling of Love and simultaneously have the intuition that I was speaking with a Krishna or a Buddha. In these moments I would feel the presence of an immensity of silence – I truly felt awed and humbled – and at the same time I couldn't help being divinely amused, as David was also childlike, playful, very human, and completely uninhibited. The net result of all this shape-shifting was that my mind suddenly let go of the need to *define* who David Spero is, and simultaneously I let go of the need to define who I am. In this letting go came great relief and a literal explosion of joy and happiness. Indeed, as my days progressed in David's happy company, I felt a deep peace and joy emerge within my heart.

The Path

Could you tell me about your spiritual awakening? That is, when did you first encounter the forces of consciousness that started to reveal to you what is beyond egoic consciousness?

My process of awakening began when I was a senior in high school. On April 26, 1975, in Providence, Rhode Island, I was initiated into an East Indian form of spiritually activated meditation. It was mantra based. That's when my spiritual life really began.

On the day I was initiated, I experienced the Transcendental Reality with remarkable clarity. For the first time in my adult life I penetrated the source of thought, the silence existing beyond the mind. From that moment on, I knew I would continue practising this form of meditation until awakening dawned.

After about one and a half years of regular meditation I began to experience the witness, which is described in classical Hindu literature as a major stage of awakening. A life beyond the superficial ego was revealed to me. Spiritual breakthroughs occurred on a daily basis. It was amazing. For about three years I lived established in the witness-position during waking, dreaming and sleep. A permanent state of detachment arose. The entire movement of my life tilted dramatically, and ecstatically, into the Transcendental Reality.

As I continued to meditate I spent more and more time in *samadhi* during meditation. In the late winter of 1979, meditation climaxed into *nirvikalpa samadhi*. I exited the top of my head and merged into the Absolute. My Self reigned supreme. I continued to meditate regularly. I even extended the duration of my meditations after nirvikalpa samadhi. I yearned for a deeper and more ecstatic spiritual union. Nirvikalpa samadhi, the witness consciousness and Self-realization all seemed incomplete. I was hungry for the impossible, the incomprehensible.

As we speak, something is happening *in consciousness.* Consciousness is activating. I am not merely conveying information. I want you to understand that. I am talking in consciousness, about consciousness, to consciousness, not merely from "me" to "you."

Okay.

We may be engaging in a dualistic conversation – there's the "me" and the "you," and they want to get to know each other – but for me, there is no separation. I really mean that. There's just consciousness.

Hallelujah.

Let's continue to dwell on consciousness. Let's invite consciousness into this moment. It's possible to share the deepest form of intimacy without control or manipulation; by just flowing into feeling, the dawning of non-dualistic awareness blossoms.

It's perfectly natural to begin speaking on a dualistic plane. Even though there's always a moon it has different phases. It comes out full on certain days of the month. It's not as if the moon ceases to be the moon by going into lesser phases of its own radiance. I use duality as a stepping stone in my teaching, not as an evil to be conquered. It's simply a part of "what is." That is my way, the way of the Mother.

When The Mother Adopts Your Nervous System

I'm interested specifically in the energetic process of awakening. In your book you speak about the divine energy, "the Mother," adopting your nervous system – that's a very interesting point to me.

Yes, this is a fascinating topic. Energetic awakening, which is to be distinguished from Transcendental Realization – what I spoke of earlier – was characteristic of my later *sadhana*. My early sadhana was meditation-based, whereas the latter was energy-based, and by energy-based I mean immersion in the *shakti* – the energetic currents in consciousness. For me, energetic awakening was rooted in the Transcendental Reality, not vice versa.

After about fifteen years of daily meditations, meditating sometimes up to six or seven hours a day, I felt compelled to visit a couple of living avatars. Both were known to be incarnations of the Divine Mother Consciousness. I meditated in their company and experienced a whole different kind of sadhana. Basically, the shakti was activated in my meditations. It opened the *nadis* and *chakras* in an almost forceful way.

I had tasted the shakti's presence occasionally in my daily meditations – the powerful vibration-current rising out of the Absolute – but now the shakti usurped my meditations. It overwhelmed my experience of the witness, dissolving my fascination with silence and detachment. Gradually my entire consciousness was transformed by this feminine energy.

Through my encounter with the shakti, the deepest form of devotion also manifested –for the Divine Mother. You could say that I became, over the next six to seven years, a devotee of the Divine Mother Consciousness. Shakti became the complete focus of my meditations from 1990-1997. I lived in my van for much of this time with my dog Blacky.

In late 1996 I was catapulted into full Unity Consciousness. Subject and object became fully transparent in the One. Only *That* existed. There was no longer an "other." All spiritual seeking ended. The Self existed on the inside and outside. Sadhana was complete.

In the late winter of 1996-1997, I stopped to rest in a Palm Springs motel. I sat to perform my daily meditation. Blacky lay at my feet, curled up asleep. On this morning my meditation quickly plummeted into Being. As the mind crossed into the Absolute I was transported into the most exquisite state of Unity Consciousness. A huge golden light erupted. Golden rays shot out of my heart, travelling in spherical waves, swallowing everything, everywhere. Golden Light circled the Earth. I held the earth like this (David holds out his arms, making a gesture embracing the Earth) – held it in my arms, so to speak. At the same time, due to my precious advaita Vedanta realization, I calmly witnessed this whole event. I remained pretty level-headed in the midst of this grandiosity.

When I left the motel that morning to have breakfast everything was bathing in a Golden Sea of Oneness. I went next door to the restaurant. The waitress brought me pancakes and I saw golden light carrying golden light. She was in golden light, and I, as golden light, prepared to eat the golden light pancakes. And in the background of my awareness, I cognized that the whole universe, seen and unseen, from the dish of pancakes to the farthest galaxy, was bathing in this same Eternal Light. It was pretty outrageous, beyond belief really, yet utterly concrete. It was as clear as you sitting before me right now.

Everything, even in their individual forms, was suffused in brilliant light. The Light was the source and energetic emanation of all living forms. This God-intoxication lasted for several days. Subjectively, I was lost in it. It was mystical. It was inebriating. I was annihilated.

Annihilated by it?

Yes, the "I" had already been dissolved permanently into the Self, but this golden vision added a new dimension of appreciation to that knowledge.

You can't experience God. God is not an object, God was not that golden light. That light was a symptom, an eruption in the vicinity of the Transcendental Consciousness. The light was a secondary wave manifestation of that essential consciousness which is beyond everything.

The light faded after a few days, but it never completely faded, you see. I have never left that state. After that, there remained a residue or *vasana* of that immensity. Vasana, by the way, comes from the root VAS, which literally means "to perfume." The vasana, or scent, or perfume, or residual ashes of that experience became the substratum of my existence, of my life. This was and is beyond all concepts. You've read in books how enlightenment goes beyond conceptualization, how the Absolute isn't a concept. I'm telling you heart to heart that I live in that state even now. My life has been exploded or imploded into that Oneness.

But to get back to my story, after a few days the Golden Light as an outer perception faded. In that fading, a tremendous energy was unleashed. *The shakti was born within that field of light.* What remained was a kind of volcanic rumbling in the depth of Being. My ability to transmit consciousness and help awaken others was born. By the way, I had no idea any of this was possible, not for me anyway. I had read about things like this in books, but when it happens *to you* – now that's a different story.

Now I can answer your question about Mother adopting my nervous system. About one year after this experience, in late 1997, I was completely taken over by Kali. By Kali, I mean the fiercest form of the shakti, personified as a Goddess-Presence. Kali-Shakti swelled into a tornado-like intensity, abducting my nervous system. Living in me, Kali also "ran" me. During this period, I remembered Ramakrishna who was possessed by the Divine Mother, dressing and acting like a woman, going into intoxicated states, acting crazy.

During this time Mother-Kali "drove" my van. Whenever She suggested going for a ride, I gasped. I knew this meant passing out at the wheel in one location and coming to in another, many miles away, not knowing what town I was in or how far I had travelled. Of course, I cannot be very precise here, only glue together scattered memories and offer as coherent a picture as possible. Much time, after all, was spent out of the mind. Driving my van, I went into samadhi for extended periods. Kali "drove" while I was "unconscious."

Kali became a fierce task-mistress. It was no fun. This went on for several months. It was maddening. Every aspect of my life was subject to Her whim. Cleaning the floor, brushing my teeth, showering, eating, sleeping – all had to be done to Her satisfaction. Everything had to be done *by* Her. There was no escape because Kali was arising as my very own mind.

What form did that energy take? I mean how…

There was no actual outer "form" of Kali.

Kali appeared within a vortex of shakti – spiritual current. She communicated with me directly through my own mind, within my own consciousness, as my own thoughts and feelings. She took over my individuality, that's all I can say. I was possessed. Adi Shankara, in his later days, prayed to Kali to inhabit Him. He implored, "let my mind become Your mind, my thoughts become Your thoughts, my *atman* become You." I experienced the fulfilment of his prayer.

So, it was your entire psychophysical existence that suddenly…

…had become Someone's plaything. That's how it felt.

You only knew that it was someone else's plaything…

I knew it was Kali, the flowering of my devotion to the Divine Mother.

Let me describe how things were at that time. I could not do anything by myself. When I needed clothes, She took me shopping and picked the shirts to buy. If I liked a shirt, I may or may not get it. She had to like the shirt. I had to have Her final permission about everything. This sounds crazy, doesn't it? She picked all colours I hated. It was terrible. At the same time, I loved every minute of it. I was enthralled, exhilarated, blissful, broken, intoxicated, crying all the time, crying because I was so intimately enamoured of this Presence.

So, there was a presence with this as well.

Yes.

An energetic presence?

Yes, arising out of my Self, out of the Absolute.

Mother Reveals The Essence Of The Four Yogas

So, what shifted?

The shift was a movement beyond advaitic Oneness into the ferocious aspect of the Divine Mother Consciousness. It was about Kali standing on the head of Shiva, about energy conquering detachment. It was about my total, irreversible transformation into the Mother. I learned to look out of Her eyes.

Odd things happened. Once I looked at a photograph of an avatar. Across her forehead passed many faces. I was totally captivated. All were Indians, some with shaved heads, and others with beards – men and women, one after the other. Mother commented that they were all my gurus from the past and that I had gone beyond them. As you can see, Mother-Kali became my Supreme Guru.

Kali tutored me through each of the four yogas described in classical Hinduism. She first instructed me to wash my tile floor. While washing it I dissolved into Pure Consciousness. Mother-Kali confirmed that this was the fulfilment of Karma Yoga, to become one with God while performing action. Next She suggested that I ask questions about anything I desired. So I asked: "Which is the higher path, knowledge or devotion?" She replied, and then I asked another question and received Her answer. After doing this three or four times my mind evaporated, and only Consciousness remained, spotless and transcendental. I experienced Jnana Yoga. Through question-and-answer and discrimination I had attained the Supreme State. She then instructed me to sit down and meditate. I sat in my chair and sank into a very deep meditation. Consciousness lifted out of my head and merged into the Self. I had transcended into the Absolute. Then consciousness descended through the head to reanimate the body. She indicated this to be the fulfilment of Raja Yoga, the "royal" yoga of meditation. To experience Bhakti Yoga Mother invited me to weep for the Divine. I wept in agony to be one with God. As I wept my whole being filled with Pure Consciousness and I dissolved into the root of feeling. My emotional body dissolved into bliss. Emerging from that sublime state Kali affirmed that I had mastered Bhakti Yoga along with all the others. I had accomplished every yoga. Actually it was She who accomplished them through me.

She went on to communicate that I could take anyone to God. Astoundingly, She insisted that I took birth in an avatar-like state. This was news to me, this avatar thing. It was not something I readily accepted. In fact, I rebelled. I thought I was just hallucinating, going mad, but She kept drilling this into me until I was utterly worn out and exhausted, until I no longer had the energy to resist. I had to accept my place in the Divine Mother Consciousness whether I liked it or not.

(Laughs) I love it! You relate all of this to me with a kind of childlike innocence that is just... it's just breathtaking. (Laughs) I hope you don't mind me giving my natural response. I think you deserve...

Just say whatever you're feeling.

You deserve to have my natural response. It's beautiful, very beautiful. Thank you for sharing it with me.

You Can't Know IT, Because You ARE IT

One time Mother-Kali instructed me to drive to the Ramakrishna Temple in Montecito, California. Driving to the temple was a real trip. I inquired of Her: "What is the origin of this world? Why did it come into being? How did manifestation itself occur?" She expressed an indifferent attitude toward the intellect's arrogance in wanting to know about these things. It was very amusing, very strange. Her attitude was, you can never know about it, because *you are it*. As I engaged Her in this dialogue, I continued to ask: "Why does duality exist? Why did duality ever come into being, since you are the One, since everything is You? What is this feeling of duality?" She responded that I should open my heart to Her energy. As I was driving up winding roads in Montecito, which is beautiful, lush, like a tropical paradise, light began to ooze out of everything, from every leaf and flower. Everything became brilliantly suffused in Divine Light. Gradually, everything dissolved into this Light. The Mother dissolved the whole physical creation and me along with it. Mother communicated something to the effect: "This is Shiva. Shiva can dissolve all this play in a second." I wept in painful ecstasy.

Finally, we arrived at the beautiful Ramakrishna Temple. A young woman sat there with an older gentleman, and he turned to her and said in a loud voice that Self-realization is very rare, very few attain it. As he spoke her back straightened as my Kundalini hit her spine. My transmission at that point filled the temple. The man didn't feel it, but she did. I stayed for a few more minutes, then hopped into my van and drove to the coast at Santa Barbara. During this time I underwent many spectacular awakenings, exhausting the whole gamut of spiritual experience.

Sahaja: Fully Embodying Consciousness

During the Enlightenment Gathering the other night – as I refer to it, the divine party – you were speaking about sahaja samadhi, the natural state. At which point did that sahaja state arise?

Sahaja samadhi arose in the midst of Kali's visit, towards its beginning.

Oh, really? Toward the beginning?

I vividly remember sitting in my studio apartment in Palm Springs, utterly relaxed into, and as, the Absolute. An incandescent spray of light issued from my body due to the soma juice or amrita that was produced within it. Soma or amrita is a natural substance produced in the body of a realized human being.

Enlightenment had evolved into sublime bodily rapture rooted in the Transcendental Consciousness. It was delicious, a merger between the Impersonal and the personal, between Consciousness and matter. The Infinite Consciousness had penetrated the density of my human body to such an extent that a milky-like spiritual lustre poured out of it.

I knew, at that point, that whatever I thought or did, even if I made mistakes, became upset or angry, even if I was sexual, no matter what I experienced I also transmitted ambrosial pure consciousness. I was immersed in *amrita sahaja samadhi* – the nectareous natural state.

It's like a childlike state?

Utterly innocent, yes, and intoxicating. Consciousness took form as the most pleasurable "liquid" and flowed through my nervous system, establishing it in a state of absolute relaxation and bliss forever.

It's just beautiful.

There are no words for it. Wordlessly intoxicating, amrita sahaja samadhi exists beyond all meditative attainments. Meditation, as a practice, could never touch this immaculate condition. I like to say that amrita sahaja samadhi describes the *embodiment of consciousness* – transparent, pure, and ambrosial – from the core of Being right to the surface of the skin.

There's one thing that I want to make clear about enlightenment. Many people are resistant to this idea, but I insist upon it: there's no difference ultimately between embodiment and Transcendental Awakening. I don't reside in some lofty, "spiritual" world and take time out to come and be with you for a while to do you a favour, and then return to my enlightenment when the nuisance of you goes away. I don't see relationship as being fundamentally different from the state of non-duality. This is the real significance of amrita sahaja samadhi, that the separative consciousness has been dissolved once and forever, not merely beyond, but into, experience.

Amrita sahaja samadhi possesses a velvety, sensuous quality. This is quite different from seeing the Self everywhere, as in my advaita Vedanta experiences. It breathes compassion.

Sahaja is all about descending, coming back down with the Light, returning to the body-mind and grabbing the sky, pulling it down over you like a sweatshirt. It's re-entering the field of pleasure and pain with magnified sensitivity and awareness.

Things Are As They Are

Thank you. I'm interested in that aspect of spiritual awakening that has led you to say things like "There's nobody here" and the sense of doer-ship being gone, when everything is just as it is.

I am happy to speak about this, but I want to first say that to talk about the non-doer or mere emptiness after amrita sahaja samadhi is like chewing on stones.

But, having said that, let's see if I can respond to your question. During my first three years of meditation, phrases like "there's nobody here" had a great deal of significance. They described the transcendence of superficial attention into its source. At the source of attention, there is no sense of "I." And as one abides in the Transcendental Consciousness the sense of doer-ship vanishes. One then witnesses action from the silence of one's own being. Silence witnesses the waking, dreaming and sleep states of consciousness.

The phrase "just as it is" opens up another spiritual vista. When things are "just as they are" a greater sense of relaxation in the Absolute happens. The sense of being the non-doer fades and one becomes more tolerant to – or shall I say united with – the field of action. At this point there's very little conceptualizing about enlightenment. You become at ease with your humanness in the Absolute. You can read the Zen Masters with full understanding. You understand when they proclaim "when eating I simply eat; when sleeping I just sleep." The seeker after enlightenment disappears.

Now, with or without a silent mind you perform action and things are just as they are. One would no longer turn nirvana into an object of pursuit. Nor do you *think of yourself* as being enlightened. You realize it's no big thing to be enlightened.

"Everything is just as it is" may also mean that Shakti or the Mother-Consciousness is running the whole show. I'd rather use the term "organic functioning" or "spontaneous functioning" to describe this final place of liberation.

Floating In And Out Of Bhavas

Sometimes you say things like, it's my Shakti and at other points during the talk you say, "I can't say it's my Shakti."

Exactly.

So, there's a flip between…

….a floating in and out of *bhavas* or divine moods. Watch a hummingbird, it has several flight patterns. Feeding on a flower it displays a particular oscillation of the wings, but when it searches for flowers it's doing a whole other thing. Still it has a different energy when it lands. In the same way, I experience various bhavas. When the Light issues out of my being, the sense of individuality dissolves completely.

What happens to the "person"…?

The "person" becomes transparent. It's *anatman*, no-self; *sunyata*, emptiness.

I just speak what I am; bhavas fluctuate.

Sometimes I'm the force of the Shakti, and that's a whole different trip – that's really wild. I just pump out this current…..

…So…

I have multiple spiritual identities or none at all. The various identities come into being as I embody different transmissions. But underneath is a vast core of emptiness. It should also be understood that these bhavas are simply labels, ideas, to help the mind understand.

Elaborate…

Elaborate? They're ideas.

I mean, it's some kind of weird oxymoron for me to say "elaborate on the nonconceptual state."

I know. It's okay. That's what makes you a good interviewer. (Silence)

I like to think of myself as ignorant rather than enlightened, because if you're enlightened you're all alone, but if you're ignorant, you have a lot of friends. You don't want to be Buddha or Christ. I mean, it's very lonely. It's best to just be among the ignorant. That's what I love about David, whoever David is. David doesn't care.

David Spero?

Yes. (pointing to his body) This. This just doesn't care whether he's a person or a non-person, whether he's exactly as he is or whether he's in conflict with himself. Spiritual identities are useless and ultimately false. He has no concern about any kind of ultimate characterization. He knows that he's like a lizard, moving out there in the desert.

When I watch those lizards I feel as if I'm one of them. I see the hawks flying, and I'm one of them. You are all of these life forms, so how can you ever define "you?" You're *everything*, not just the pure consciousness of the Absolute. You're not just that which is beyond everything – the non-doer. You're all life forms playing in this field of perception that we call "world." David is all of it, and he is none of it.

What you are describing seems devastating.

Actually, I don't know how I'm alive after all that I've been through; one massive awakening after another. They've taken their toll on this body-mind, but it has survived. Obviously I was meant to live through all of that and carry the perfume, the ultimate vasana, the ultimate fragrance of the Divine, which is beyond all knowledge. It's something that no one knows about. You don't know about it, I don't know about it. We're like innocent children before it.

The Divine itself?

Yes, it's beyond subject and object, beyond knowledge. "Divine" is a metaphorical term for that energy which is *running through* everything. The "Divine" or "God" is not merely "above" or "under" or "within" or "beneath" a life form. The concept of the Divine as a location or place is a fanciful idea created by theologians, a meaningless term intimately bound to a philosophy of being saved or rescued by a Supreme Being. It's related to the notions of faith and belief, notions that breed a multitude of violent, religious hypocrites. The Divine is a concept generated in fear – the fear that we have been abandoned by life.

In actuality you are a single life form imbedded in an atmosphere swimming with billions of other life forms, all equally blind to their source. Through organic intelligence the human functions, simply and spontaneously, just like everything else. But remember, the human being is no better than a lizard or a hummingbird. It's nothing exalted, nothing special. Certainly, it does not exist on a platform of moral or ontological superiority, as the Western religions have suggested. Western man has borne a great inferiority complex, which requires him to create a bully God to exalt him above the rest of nature. Enlightenment is seeing through all that theological nonsense. After all the arrogant religious concepts have been eradicated, awakening may occur.

We don't know *anything*. Don't ever think you're better than a lizard or a hummingbird. You're no improvement. In fact, there is every good reason to believe the opposite, that the human being is an evolutionary defect.

Why a defect?

Because there is something terribly perverse about the way the current human being functions. He is trashing the planet. He doesn't understand that the world is sacred. Earth is a paradise.

We are not here as the result of sin or karma, because the reincarnation process somehow has dumped us into a human body. We're here because super-affluent energy has birthed us. Don't believe anything the religions have said – they're all full of shit. Don't believe anything any religion has said about original sin, karma, your being here because of your vasanas, that you've taken birth because you've been ignorant.

We are here to enjoy. Sure, suffering occurs, but we are here to taste the ecstasy we were born out of.

Speaking About The Earth

Well, I wanted to ask about the planet, so…

I mean, just look at Los Angeles. It has a perfect climate. You can grow anything there. It doesn't snow. The ocean is there, but it's extremely polluted. In Malibu and Venice there are signs saying don't go in the water, it's too toxic.

Los Angeles should have dozens of huge sprawling parks, many square miles in area, where people can walk and hike and be. It should have thousands of organic farms. Instead, the city is an endless chaos of steel and concrete, ugly and polluted. We're talking about one of the most beautiful pieces of land on the planet. Human beings don't know how to cherish, how to work with the energies of this world.

We destroyed the Native American cultures. The Indians had a great sense of union with the land. We obliterated them with alcohol and disease. The Europeans brought with them their ugly, violent Christianity and lust for gold. The aboriginal peoples had knowledge they could have shared with us; if we had opened our minds, our hearts, there could have been a great merger. This is a perfect example of why human beings continue to devolve. When the Europeans came here to America, they had the perfect opportunity to learn from a superior culture. Instead, what did they do? They systematically purged and eradicated a culture, one that lived without any form of dangerous technology. The Native Americans respected and loved nature. They adored it. We weren't evolved enough to dialogue with them. We're still not.

Human beings still want to conquer each other rather than lovingly cooperate. Ecologically we're in big trouble and it's just a question of time when global warming will *really hit*, this year or next year or a few years from now. I don't like where we're heading. My energy may help to rectify the behaviour of human beings, although that doesn't seem to be happening on a large scale. The fundamentalist Christian church down the street, which celebrates the destruction of the planet as part of its idiotic, apocalyptic faith, draws over a thousand people, while ten to fifteen come to sit with me. So, there aren't enough serious people, people who are seeking intelligent spiritual development. That's the only thing that's really going to help at this point, the only thing that will help us realize that the environment is inherently sacred and that the promise in an afterlife, where some are saved and others damned, is precisely what makes human beings behave so ugly toward this earth and to one another.

Spontaneous Functioning

When we were outside just now on our walk, I kind of playfully asked you, "What is enlightenment?" and your obviously spontaneous answer was, "in back of me, above me, below me, around me, but never in me, not me." Let's go deeper into that. It reminds me of Meister Eckhart.

Meister Eckhart loved talking about the Oneness. Some of his writings are beautiful.

You can't really say what enlightenment is or what it feels like to be enlightened. That was the meaning of my response. Enlightenment, as the term is generally used, refers to a subjective experience. It certainly touches human subjectivity, but also goes beyond it. Enlightenment is not merely on the inside of the human being. Enlightenment is transpersonal, a style of functioning in which the feeling of separation has been dissolved. You see, you may call it a style of functioning or a mode of consciousness. It's both.

Nature exhibits *enlightened functioning* everywhere, not individually enlightened creatures. Animals, insects, fish and reptiles act without any illusory centre, without the "me." A Zen master once pointed to a stick smeared with shit as the Buddha-nature. We were just in nature together. We stood in front of those beautiful mountains. Everything in nature is a spontaneous happening. Lizards, birds and insects are not in "states;" they simply function. So, too, an enlightened human being may be liberated into spontaneous functioning, into that same energy that is going on everywhere else in nature. It's a great mystery how spontaneous functioning comes into being. How a person reverts to that is a mystery. We don't know how that happens, there's no explanation. Therefore when spiritual people say, "I'm getting enlightened," that's a mistake, because they are just referring to the dissipation of ignorance. That's what people often mean by the word enlightenment. When they claim to be illumined or are becoming illumined, they are still describing the diminishing of ignorance. When an aspirant begins to awaken and light starts to shine through, he becomes excited and makes premature claims about "being enlightened." But if that light were to penetrate totally, then he would *be* that light. At first this awakening would be overwhelming, but later on it would fade into the background, never to be forgotten.

Enlightenment is not a thing or an idea. It cannot be possessed or made useful. The human being is cunning. It wants to turn everything into an object, into something useful. But that's not what enlightenment is about. It's a trans-utilitarian consciousness. It's about becoming innocent again. So, you learn how to function in primal simplicity, with "no-mind." You've heard that expression.

Can you go into that further? That is, what is "no-mind?"

You can't say *what* no-mind is; you can only say: no-mind *is*.

It resists scrutiny.

How so?

Well, it's sacred; it's in its own dimension. This is what makes it beautiful, what makes it holy. What makes it God is that you can't take it apart.

Even the most brilliant philosophical minds cannot penetrate "no-mind." It's love, beyond question and answer – undiluted feeling. (Silence) It's only during the breakthroughs that you think "Oh, I'm beyond ignorance" or "I am the Self." That's all part of waking up, but later on, when you get over that, you reside in a place that is neither ignorant nor awakened. Ignorance and awakening are just words.

The key is to reside in nothingness until you're utterly released from the sense of self. You become silenced, obliterated through deep meditation. Then, it's as if, in that nothingness, the body is made translucent, becomes porous and thousands of microfractures appear. Your body – gross body, subtle body – radiates this Light out of every pore. You identify with the Light but you do not attach to It. It's not your possession. It's in everything.

I never consider talking about this kind of thing. I'm talking about it with you now because you're asking me. When nobody's here interviewing me, I don't even think about it, except when I teach.

Meditation Is Just Living Naturally

What is meditation for you?

Meditation is that experience which takes the individual consciousness back to the ocean of Universal Being. It can be learned formally from a teacher or lineage. It can also be grasped intuitively, spontaneously, within oneself. There are many forms of meditation, many excellent forms that carry the transmissions of their founders or gurus. A legitimate form of meditation is one that is spiritually activated with the realization of its teacher or lineage. If a human being is attentive, life will instruct her at some point on how to meditate. Meditation may happen while looking at a beautiful sunset. It happens spontaneously whenever one is transfixed by beauty. Whatever cultivates care, compassion, sensitivity, subtlety, calmness, patience, appreciation and an expanded sense of being is meditation.

Sitting with an Awakened Master is also meditation, much more than that really. At the very least meditation will be activated in the consciousness of one who sits with an Awakened Master. The Master's Kundalini will stimulate, and accomplish the whole path of meditation. In other words, the Shakti performs the meditation.

Ultimately, meditation is a state of being; it's just living naturally with what is. Meditation is looking closely at things, not taking them for granted. It is being ready to open up completely at any moment to something that comes into your field of attention, looking at it with depth. Meditation is the capacity for total relationship. There is no special secret here, no esoteric knowledge. Meditation is what is happening now.

What do you mean?

Meditation is radiating and spilling into this interaction right now, it's engulfing us. There's nothing that I'm not showing you. I don't reserve something special for myself to relish that's beyond human interaction. I don't have to run away from human noise to feel the power and presence of meditation. Once I meditated to reach enlightenment, but all of that seems like illusion now.

I have no actual teaching, even though I pretend to teach.

Everyone Is Presumed Innocent

What prompts you to pretend to teach?

(Silence) The feeling that cares for everything. For me, there's no problem or dilemma in consciousness, but for some people there seems to be. When I sit with people, I assume everyone's enlightened. When they walk in I presume they are awake, Buddhas coming to enjoy sacred company. And they are all presumed innocent until they indicate otherwise.

Presumed innocent?

Innocent until they indicate they're in some kind of bondage, overwhelmed by some suffering or joy. Once they show me this, I begin to work with them energetically in consciousness. "My" transmissions begin to spontaneously activate for them – *for them*! They're not for "me," they're not "my" transmissions; they happen through this body-mind, but they represent a reality that is greater than it.

We're all born with nervous systems capable of realising the Transcendental Consciousness. Once in a while nature generates a body-mind with extraordinary transmission-power. I was born like this. As I mentioned previously, I did meditate for many years, enjoying many awakenings. But I was never satisfied with any kind of spiritual experience. Every awakening, no matter how extraordinary, was superfluous to who and what I really was. I ascended into many mystical and intoxicating states. In fact, I was an addict for spiritual intoxication. That was my only joy, to keep plummeting into consciousness, first going down into the dark recesses of Being and later being swallowed completely by the Light. Over time, my inherent oneness with the Divine was revealed. My process eventually fulfilled itself and the transmissions of Divine Light, Divine Love and Kundalini-shakti were born. I carried these transmissions the way a mother carries milk. I say "I" carry them, but there is really no room for the "I" when you are talking on this exalted level.

No Splinter Of Separation

What do you mean there's no room for the "I"?

Let's talk about being free from the "I."

There's a superficial form of Advaita Vedanta circulating these days. It claims that the source of the "I" is the Absolute and only "That" needs to be realized. That realization, according to this philosophy, encompasses the beginning and end of enlightenment. A kind of disjointed state is epitomized in which the body, mind and emotions are *witnessed* from a superior viewpoint. This, believe it or not, is purported to be the highest state of awakening. This new "pop" advaita Vedanta movement often invokes the names of Ramana Maharishi or Nisargadatta Maharaj to justify itself. It lures aspirants with an entirely impersonal realization, one that has been freed from the trap of the "me" and all its human entanglements. What was once "sin" for the Christian has become "mind" or "ego" for the neo-advaita Vedantist. They view the relative personality as some sort of burdensome husk to be overcome through Transcendental Realization. Students are instructed to keep remembering Consciousness, the source of the "I," so that the ego-sense merges into the Self once and for all.

You know the myth of Sisyphus. This sort of sadhana never ends, nor does it ever quite succeed. It has been going on in India, and around the world in other forms, for centuries. These anti-body, anti-feeling, anti-mind, anti-ego teachings are nothing new. They were created by men to shield themselves from vulnerability and insure the domination of patriarchal views. The human urge to love and be loved, relationships, are serious problems in these teachings. They, along with the ego, must be obliterated.

According to my understanding, in full realization every aspect of human functioning *arises out of* the Absolute. I definitely acknowledge the necessity to transcend the "I," totally, but I also acknowledge the existence of a limited identity after realization of the Self. The small "I" continues to arise after enlightenment, like a wave in the sea, as does the mechanism of desire – desire continues, desire lingers. So the very highest state is a profound relaxation in which silence and action, transcendence and desire are wedded.

In the end there's no room, no space between THAT and whatever else you consider yourself to be, no splinter of separation between *every aspect of you and That. (Phone rings.)*

Do you want to get it?

No, it's probably a political phone call. (Long silence) It's nice just being here; we don't even have to say anything. (Someone leaves message on answering machine, which turns out to be an invitation to a funeral. Then, long silence.) This is very important – you don't need to do anything, nor seek for anything. The mind is stubborn. Even after enlightenment it still wants to seek, running after teachers and holy places.

(Sings) Nityananda.....Nityananda (At this point a deep joy that had been welling up in my heart literally burst, and I found a spontaneous chant issuing from my lips.)

Is that your favourite song?

(Laughs) I have no idea (Keeps singing)

Nitya means what?

Eternal bliss. Nitya is eternal and Ananda is bliss.

The advaita Vedanta fundamentalists get angry when you speak of bliss, because they think you're ascribing a quality to the Absolute, but the inherent nature of the Absolute is happiness, and therefore it can be called bliss — there's no problem calling it bliss.

Mother Takes Away All The States, And Then All The States Are You

During the talk the other day, you spoke about the Mother as being the energy that is everywhere and within everything. It evoked a beautiful sense of the Mother. You know, when I think about someone like Sri Bhagawan Nityananda, it's obvious that the Para Kundalini in him is fully flowered, and to me, the Mother is the total flowering. It's when the individual Kundalini in a body-mind organism unfolds itself and becomes active, such that it merges into the universal field of energy, and the nature of that energy is one with its Source. So, the vibration of consciousness is one with the ground of being in which it arises. What is your understanding of the Mother?

The Mother is that energy which eradicates delusion and reintegrates the human being with the whole of nature. The Mother bestows, ultimately, the blessing of amrita sahaja samadhi, the nectar-like natural state. That describes it as a definition, but to understand the Mother experientially you must first relax into pure consciousness, so that the boundary between the relative and Absolute melts. In that non-dual relaxation, amrita or soma juice is secreted in the nervous system, an inebriating "liquid." Some refer to this substance as *amrita nadi*, the current of ambrosia. This exquisite transformation happened, for me, after all advaita Vedanta-style realizations, after there was nothing more to gain or lose spiritually. Beyond all grandiose realizations, including *aham brahamasi*, which means "I am God, I am the Absolute," a subtle nectar is produced to heal the human nervous system in the state of enlightenment. Advaita Vedanta realizations are magnificent, and in some sense supreme, but they begin to look like peanuts when the body is dissolved into the glowing radiance of amrita sahaja samadhi. The taste of that fusion is indescribable as the body itself is turned into devotional nectar.

Mother possessed my nervous system in order to inebriate it, to usher it into a deeper form of awakening. To do this I had to become Her plaything, whisked around by Her Whims. What She required was my total disappearance into Her. This complete surrender was something She accomplished with Her ferocious Energy. The Mother, as Kali, descended upon me with all Her wrath and love.

After the sahaja samadhi?

Amrita sahaja samadhi was created *during* Kali's visit. It was an exquisite moment of awakening which produced a new kind of samadhi, but truly it was the end of all samadhis. It was the height of Divine Experience in a human nervous system.

After amrita sahaja samadhi Mother-Kali usurped every aspect of my life. She turned it upside down and inside out. And She did this without ethics, without morals. To say I was humiliated completely and then exalted absolutely describes Her final work during this time. My existence had to be reduced to a state of pure, simple, mindless functioning. You can use words like God-consciousness or enlightenment, but they don't scratch the surface of this experience. I like to say that Kali possessed me; that's about the best description I can give. Yet, it was so much more than that, a fantastic voyage from the surface of the body to the ends of the universe and back. I encountered a most wrathful and loving form of the Divine Mother, the Light of lights and the blackest of darkness. These extremes were embedded into my own human functioning. Everything I did during this time was Her doing. Everything I thought was Mother's thinking. Everything I wished for was Mother's wish. I wanted to escape but I couldn't. Looking back at this now, it was psycho-spiritual madness. It was the total breakdown of everything about the human.

I continue to transmit the elixir-like radiance of amrita sahaja samadhi and other forms of spiritual transmission. I've come to realize that every state, enlightened and ignorant, every samadhi and every form of nascence, are in me and that I am in them. This is total freedom, unimaginable liberation – and bondage too. So Mother takes away all the states and then the states are you.

I love to meet all types of spiritual seekers, Karma yogis, Bhakti yogis, Jnana yogis, Raja yogis, those who crave to realize God. I even adore those who hate God or care less about God's existence. I can work with anyone who is sincere, anyone at all. You've asked me what the Mother is: it's that capacity to be available to anybody, to everybody, without conditions.

To thoroughly answer your question, though, Mother has been several things to me. Avatars I've encountered, the Deity that abducted me in Palm Springs, nature, and ultimately the Source of All.

Mother is just a word for the inexpressible movement of life itself.

There's Something Functioning Which Is bigger Than Any of Us

In your process, in the final analysis…

(Laughs) Yeah…?

Tell me?

There's no process. There's no "me." There's nothing there. There's something functioning that is bigger than any of us.

Essentially, in my teaching work, I baby-sit. I entertain. At this fun gathering the Otherness comes to do its Work.

Tell me a little more about your teaching work.

There's not much to say, really. Even my own understanding and description of what I do is limited – not of much use. It's too big to be understood, but it can be felt. In any event, when I describe my Work using words I have only summarized my process. My memory has fed upon certain labels that it was taught. Everything I say is in the field of conditioning. Every word comes from a borrowed source; there's no original word, unless we start making up words. In that case we can just babble infinite nothingnesses to each other.

(Laughs)

I can't think anything that hasn't already been thought. When you taste the sacredness that's beyond time and space, it's like the breaking of an ocean wave along the California coast – a big spray of meaningless bliss and energy, issuing into the relative like a wind blowing from an unknown source. The Absolute, moving within itself, surges into time and space to produce a sensation of bliss for sentient beings.

Oh, and by the way – don't let me forget. This is all bullshit. All this talk, it has no meaning. You'll never get at the truth with me.

Tell me more about the natural state, what that state of functioning is like. Tell me more about what you were speaking to me about on the telephone, and what you've said in these interviews about the lizards.

The natural state happens after you've penetrated your conditioning and a certain part of the brain has been shocked into pure consciousness. If you can strip the mind, make it totally naked, coax it through all its fears and inhibitions, pleasures and pains, it gets into a movement that's similar to the consciousness of animals – an energy which is both silent and active.

And so, a person who's in the natural state lives literally like a frog or an insect! It's difficult to imagine this, going beyond society's prejudices, going beyond religious superstitions. That's where you finally reside – if you can talk about residing there. I am describing a state where your own energy has subsided; the will has been cracked, thrown into the trash. Most people depend totally on willpower to function. You know that. All I can say is: observe a lizard, observe a bird, observe it very carefully, or observe a bee. You see how these beings move; their intellect doesn't come into play, saying, "I'll do this" and then they do it. There's no separation at all between the doer and the doing. The doer and the doing are exactly the same. It becomes complicated when you bring a human being into that state, a human who has a different brain, one that creates the sensation of past, present, and future – and therefore chooses. That is where it becomes strange. Because now you have someone who can apparently adopt the attitude of separation within a non-divisive consciousness. This is very interesting because we can, even with total spontaneity, say "I think I'll sit down and take a break." And even though it's an idea, and it's conceptual, and it's even apparently willed, that "willed" act happens spontaneously.

There is no way to describe what enlightenment is or is not after a certain point. That's a fact. In the end you actually "lose" your own enlightenment, you just return to delusion. That's the final return, the final mind blower. You cannot separate into a Self-realized posture forever.

Tell me about that?

The final movement in the spiritual journey is when your own enlightenment ceases to be an object of your own fascination. It no longer provokes any reaction in your mind even about its own presence. You become totally ignorant. I'm talking about innocence here, the innocence that doesn't distinguish between this and That, between Consciousness and matter; you become sublimely innocent.

Do you ever feel depressed, bored?

Yes, of course.

Lonely…

Lustful, lonely, depressed, upset, in fact, probably more than most people.

Why more?

Because I don't dilute feelings, I don't play with them. I am unable to disassociate from anything.

You don't dilute…

… with some kind of positivist philosophy or spiritual belief.

Is that like the ground of being that allows everything to arise?

You say it's the ground of being, but I am afraid that we are going to get into some kind of spiritual pep talk. You know what a pep talk is.

Like a coaching session.

Yeah, like "Come on, guys! We're gonna go out there and win!" There is no "Ultimate Reality," superior, free and untouched. We are talking about spontaneous functioning. We want to be careful with phrases such as "the Ground of Being" or "the Ultimate Reality," because those terms tend to create hopeful illusions in the human mind. It's best to revert to a language of simplicity, like spontaneous functioning, and look at the lives of animals and insects to understand how an enlightened person *functions*.

Can you elaborate?

There are notions about the "me" being bound or enlightened. Those notions must be seen through.

First, you have to reach the point where you're glimpsing Pure Consciousness freely and deeply. Pure Consciousness is that non-cognitive space where thought cannot enter. Once you find that connection, the key is to abide in it, relate to it. Abide in it day and night. As you're surrendering into It, you will realize something incredible – that you have been drawn back into the source of everything. Paradoxically, after a certain amount of realization, the source will fling you right back into the body. Then spontaneous functioning has come into being.

How is it that at that point the spontaneous functioning comes into being?

There's no more "how," no more "why." (Silence) Once I speak, it's gone.

Tell me about that.

It's happening now. (Long silence)

What is self in your understanding?

(Long silence) The self is Absolute Being, but there is no self that knows this. The Self knows itself from within its Self. Simultaneously, the self is everything that it does. When you're making coffee, you're a coffee-making-self; when you're having sex, you're a sexing-self; when you're eating, you're an eating-self. You're just moment to moment what you are. Of course, if you were to analyse and compare these statements, we have more problems again, right?

What is consciousness in your understanding? What is consciousness, and we can take that however it occurs to you. How do you want to respond to the word "consciousness?"

It depends upon your point of view. On the one hand, consciousness means the known, the knower, and the process of knowing. In this case it's relative. But you can also write "Consciousness" with a capital "C," meaning Being or the Self. Consciousness retains both meanings for me. You see what I mean by that?

My response would be yes, without thinking about it.

You speak about relationship. You said to me that it isn't in opposition to what is.

Yes.

What is that? Tell me about that.

In relationships we are bound. As the Self we are free. We are both. That's the paradox. We live, not in one box or the other, but in both realities simultaneously. That simultaneity is what I mean by relationship. I'd rather not say that "I am free" the way it's used in advaita Vedanta. It's not that I don't understand that kind of talk. But the kind of freedom they are pointing to encourages disassociation from relationships. I am not "free." That's all I want to say. I am definitely not free. I don't like that kind of talk. After all, if you're free then you're free from something, which means that your freedom is based on separation.

When you hear the word freedom...?

. . . I'm bound, like everything else. I'm bound like the lizard, like the fly and the bee. They're all bound intensely to their forms but they function beautifully within them. There's not a trace of defect in the way a fish swims, and yet it ends up in the mouth of another fish. Has it made a mistake? I don't think so. I don't know.

One thing that strikes me about you is that you often refer to "innocence;" it keeps occurring to me that you're like a one-year-old.

Not even one, right? I could be even half of that. Maybe I've never even been born.

(Laughs a lot) (At this stage my whole body felt as if freed into a luminous release and ease, resting and floating in a sea of Light and Joy as spontaneous yogic movements began to happen of their own accord.)

You're having kriyas. You're having yogic kriyas. That's good – now you're a lizard.

Oh, yeah.

Everything in nature performs kriyas, spontaneous movements. The nervous system is finally behaving spontaneously. It's as if someone had been tied up and the teacher's transmission cut the ropes. Inhibitions are released.

When I was immersed in Kali-consciousness, it was one unending kriya. I did many crazy things. Kali instructed me to give away all my clothes. I gave them all to charity. I had nothing left in my closets, nothing. One day a friend came to visit and he felt sorry for me. He saw that I had nothing. He said, "Here, take this, borrow this for a while." It was a beautiful CD player. He gave it to me with some CDs. After he left I asked the Mother,

"Do you like this?" She responded, "No, we're giving it away." I argued: "No, I will not do that! This was a gift." She communicated, "That's all good and fine, and now we're giving it away." We drove to the local thrift shop and donated it to charity.

Is that how she said it, "It's all good and fine?"

Yes, something like that. She didn't care.

My friend came by the next day to ask how I liked the player. I said, "Mother gave it away; she gave it to charity." He just turned around and walked out. After he left, Mother commented that the CD player had bad energy and we did him a favour by giving it away. She then led me to buy him a new one, which I did. I gave it to my friend and said, "Mother bought you this new one, and She's sorry She gave the other one away." It turned out that the one she gave away belonged to him and his partner, who had died recently of AIDS. There was a lot of sorrow attached to that object.

Wow, that's beautiful. So you would mention to people what was going on? Were you candid about this? Did anyone think you were crazy?

Yes, with him I was candid. He thought I was crazy after I did that. Today we're still good friends. He understands who I am now.

Outwardly, were you concerned about what people thought of you?

No, that's the essential point. I had really been released from the self image.

Kali Took The In-dweller

During the Kali period Mother rode with me in my van. We drove around New Mexico, Arizona and California. On one occasion near Santa Barbara I stopped on the side of the highway overlooking the ocean. There I went into a deep samadhi, the most profound one of my life. I left my body, my spirit floating out of my head.

Like a transcending?

No, this was deeper. I was leaving the body for good. A very thin cord held my spirit to my body. As my spirit rose I suddenly felt a jolt of fear in my solar plexus that interrupted the dying process and whisked me back into the body. It was the urge to love and be loved that pulled my spirit back down. That's the only reason I came here – to love.

When you went up and out, what was your sense of what you are, who you are?

There was no time for that. It was like the in and out of a breath, just a spontaneous leaving. There was nothing else. I ascended higher and higher into nothingness and swirling, rainbow-like colours, everything receding underneath me. I was dying. Only a very thin cord kept me connected to the body. When I sensed the cord was about to snap I became terrified. I saw how far this movement had progressed. At that point I consciously and spontaneously interrupted my dying process. Perceiving I wasn't coming back, in an instantaneous "Ah!" (gasp,) my spirit descended from the Absolute down into my crown and reanimated the body. For several days I was terrified to close my eyes. Death was breathing down my neck. I had to make a conscious effort to stay in the body.

Wow.

Even if I closed my eyes for several seconds I felt death returning, coming back to scoop me up.

As I continued to drive the ascending current of shakti coming out of my head caused the metal roof of my van to crackle. The heat, energy and light were apparently, on a very subtle level, actually dissolving the metal in the roof of my van. Different odors arose; my van smelled like a pine box coffin. It was an olfactory metaphor for the complete death of David.

Did you have that sense of the metaphor?

Yes, I thought I would die, but Mother-Kali kept me alive. She gave me direct insight into the nature of my birth, which came out of the Absolute. That is what I had to see and accept.

You could say that Kali took the in-dweller in order to give me these experiences and knowledge. She ate and then regurgitated a completely new David, one who would finally accept this new avatar-like position, and function and teach within it. Ironically, I was fully established in Unity Consciousness the previous year, but through Kali's fierce lessons I learned to abide in a new way. Do you see how devastating this was?

You said I was an enigma. This is what you're sensing. *This* is an enigma (pointing to his body.) It has been confounded, not awakened.

Kali destroyed me with one hand and caressed me with the other to remove every spiritual identity, except the one I was born in. It was heaven and hell. I cried buckets of tears. Pleasure and pain, liberation and bondage, up and down, in and out were obliterated in Her fiery love. You asked me whether people noticed. I guess they did. I don't know. I didn't care. I was driving most of the time. Once in a while I ate.

How much did you eat?

Not much. Once in Arizona Kali steered me to a pizza place and we had lunch. That lunch was like a feast. After that it was back into the van.

During this time I experienced all kinds of things, subtle apparitions, demons, gurus, energies, presences. Once at dusk I saw a *rakshasa*, a particular demon described in the Rig Veda. On another occasion, we drove to a remote area in central Arizona. In the distance the sun was setting. I steered my van over to the side of the road for an unobstructed view of the sun. Mother guided me to look briefly at the sun. An amazing thing occurred. As I was gazing into it, a piece of the sun fractured into a fragment and shot directly into my forehead, into my sixth chakra, like a bullet. I felt a cool burning sensation and realized that the sun dwelt in me. The sun merged into me the way a drop merges into a pool of water.

During this time, I begged Kali to leave me alone. The part of me that wanted to be left alone was the part that Kali deconstructed. I could not defend myself against Her. I was like a lion cub in the mouth of its mother – big teeth that could break me at any moment, but they never broke me. She carried me through all my primal terror and bliss.

I'll share one other remarkable thing that happened in Southern California. My van was running out of gas. I stopped at a self-service station. Kali had cancelled all of my credit cards. None of them worked. Here I was in the middle of nowhere, with no gas, no cash and no credit cards. Mother came to me internally and said to check my fanny pack for cash. I checked it. There was nothing in there, not a dime. She said to check again. When I looked again I found a large handful of shiny new coins. These coins had been manifested out of nothing. She told me to count them. The coins totalled about two dollars and I purchased enough gas to get home.

That ferocious manifestation of the Mother, is all that just history now?

Not exactly. Mother-Kali as task-mistress eventually faded, but the actual flavour of the Divine Mother Consciousness continues. A kind of sweetness which I'd rather call amrita sahaja samadhi has replaced the ferocious Kali. And the other aspects of the Divine Mother Consciousness – Lakshmi, Saraswati and Durga – they function as wish-fulfilling trees, granting boons and helping others.

It is David that is just history now. Whatever he is, it's a mystery. In any event, the resting in amrita sahaja samadhi is not something that happens to an individual; it is not for "the me," nor can it be understood with separative awareness – whatever this is.

Whatever this is… (laughs.) So, what was that like, that year, just functioning and being the functioning? Being the desire for a meal? Being the desire for a bed? Being?

David has been deconstructed into the shakti. That's what exists now, what you're talking to. I am what I do. It's very strange. Talking about this is a big bag of contradictions, but it is lived without knowledge or effort.

Transmission: The Perfume Of The Mother

What is a bag of contradictions?

Living, living this and teaching. What could there possibly be to teach? Now only a kind of organic functioning remains, or the Mother, if you prefer that term. The Mother is. She's available to all. That's the beauty, that's the offering. The radiation of Mother's Grace has nothing to do with what I subjectively experience. Sometimes I'm in a grouchy mood and I'm critical when I teach. Other times I'm very sweet like a little child, loving, tender and playful. Sometimes I'm like a madman, and there are times I don't say anything. A couple of weeks ago a great silence ate up everything. We just looked at each other without anything to say. Everyone was transported, intoxicated. I don't know why they all became intoxicated. After all, I'm just a body sitting in a chair with all those other bodies sitting in chairs. You see my point? When I asked them about this, they describe the reception of various transmissions.

Let me say more about this. Through my teaching work I've learned that there are four major types of spiritual transmission. There is the transmission of Light. Light transmission leads you to the Transcendental Consciousness or silence of Absolute Being. It brings the realization that *you are THAT*. Some aspirants have described the room dissolving into white or golden light.

The second transmission is of radiant feeling or pure love. Some people sit and cry. Their hearts come open, shattered into wide-open-feeling. A few weeks ago another said, "David, when I sit with you there's nothing but Divine Love. Half the time I don't hear you speaking, but my heart widens into pure feeling." Love, devotion, worship, adoration, passion, appreciation, affection – all of these together make up the second transmission.

The third mode of transmission is energy or Shakti – the spiritual currents that emerge out of the Absolute. They ascend and descend throughout the aspirant's consciousness, opening all the chakras. Shakti is simply the vibratory aspect of the Absolute, a voracious current of raw energy.

The final transmission is the multi-dimensional lights in consciousness, which occur in the sixth chakra primarily during meditation. These color frequencies heal the nervous system in subtle ways, helping the recipient to adjust to the new levels of consciousness that are glimpsed.

Manifestations, would you call them?

Yes, manifestations.

How do you relate to those subtle phenomena?

I don't relate to them. Most of the time I don't even experience them. They are not for me; they are for others.

The Perfume of the Mother?

Yes, you may call it that. I should also mention, in this context, that many people report smelling sweet fragrances when we sit together in meditation. The room fills with the scent of flowers or unburnt incense. These transmissions and this scent are the perfumes of the Mother Consciousness.

Graces?

Grace. Yes, absolutely. These phenomena are happening through me, but quite beyond me. Are you getting the picture now? That body sitting up there, it's human, it's finite. You can touch it; it drinks, it eats. It craves touch like every other body in the room. I don't want to fall into the trap of insisting that these graces are not me. I don't want to play advaita-inspired "not-me" word games to sound politically correct. What I want to say is that the physical body is precious as it becomes permeated in cosmic bliss. I don't possess any mock humility about this. The body too can become God. The physical body may become so suffused in Light that the Self comes right through it. It's not just the inner Self that's God. But if you ask me who I am, I really don't know. There's some sort of protection that prevents me from knowing. I cannot look into that immensity even though it's my very own Self, nor can I be certain, in a conventional sense, that I am "enlightened."

You can't do it?

It's not allowed. It's not possible.

During the Kali phase, I picked up a copy of the *Tao Te Ching*. I read the first poem:

The Tao that can be told is not the eternal Tao.
The name that can be named is not the eternal name.
The nameless is the beginning of heaven and earth....

As I was reading, that state of consciousness dawned, the silence, the void beyond time and space. My whole being took on the meaning of that Taoist poem. In that moment, I *knew* that I was all of the scriptures, every God and Goddess. I was beyond all of them. I put the book down with tears in my eyes.

Swami Shankaracharya

Introduction
The Eternal Unity Of Shiva And Shakti

Swami Shankaracharya, born Steve Sabine, was blessed with the direct realization he refers to as, "God Alone Is" in 1981, while on pilgrimage in India. Previously, Steve had been working in the field of aerospace engineering. During this period felt a deep yearning to directly experience God. This yearning evolved into an all-consuming quest that eventually led him to serve two great masters of Kundalini Mahayoga: Baba Muktananda and Dhyanyogi Madhusudandasji. In the presence of these masters, he found himself undergoing profound Kundalini awakening and during several years of intense spiritual discipline, progressed into advanced stages of mystical awareness. This culminated in the unbroken experience of undifferentiated Oneness (Parasamvit,) ending the fluctuation between the ecstasy of God and the turmoil of the world. The energy of Consciousness appeared to him in the form of the Divine Mother of the universe, giving him the command: "Bring my teachings to the West."

Shankaracharya draws on the rich spiritual heritage of the ancient traditions to express his awakening and teaching. He was given the name Shankaracharya by Dhyanyogi after taking Tantric Sannyas (monkhood) and initiation into the formal practices of Divine Mother worship by Ramesh Moudgil. Ramesh is a Tantric master in a long line of Shakta adepts. Interestingly, this initiation into the formal Tantric path took place *after* Shankaracharya's awakening into the Supreme.

My own association with Swami Shankaracharya spans many years, during which time we occasionally corresponded via mail and spoke on the phone. Then, coincidentally, while I was on pilgrimage in India, I ran into Shankaracharya, who was also on pilgrimage, thus meeting him personally for the first time. I was deeply moved by the pure radiance of divine

Presence that shone in his eyes. Our eyes seemed to lock, and I found myself unable to break his gaze. I thought, *How could I look away from this pure Light?* I literally perceived that I was looking into the eyes of the Supreme, as if through those eyes shone an ocean of light. That afternoon, I returned to my hotel room and lay on the bed, absorbed in the scintillating field of Shakti, the activity and presence of which had been quickened by my meeting with Shankaracharya. I understand each such energetic encounter to be both a glimpse of a deeper level of revelation and also a purifying process. During the influx of energy, subtle blockages in the sushumna (the subtle counterpart to the human spine wherein the awakened life energy flows) are removed by the sheer force of the energetic flow. The result is a deeper experience of the inner Self.

Shankaracharya has been giving Shaktipat initiation in the West for many years and is the head of Sadhana Ashram where he resides. The ashram is currently in the process of relocating within California. It is dedicated to the Divine Mother and the awakening of the Kundalini Shakti. Shankaracharya has developed a profound teaching that marries the eternal unity of Being with the eternal becoming of the world, a teaching unsurpassed in its clarity and beauty. He has guided many seekers during their own inner awakenings and this contact with western seekers over the years has allowed him to refine his teaching greatly. What impresses me most is Shankaracharya's integration of the notion of self-improvement within the broader understanding that all is unfolding perfectly according to divine Will. He sees a very valid and even necessary place for concerted effort to refine oneself on a personal level *within* the vaster perspective of the eternal oneness and perfection of Being.

During my stay in Topanga, where his Ashram was presently located, we called in to the Zen Zoo Café for tea, where we engaged in some penetrating discussions on the nature of spiritual awakening. At one point, I vividly recall Shankaracharya smacking his hand on the table, and with deep passion expressing, "This *is* the eternal Subject." Thus, he was expressing the eternal unity of Being and becoming, the mystical truth that the objectless Awareness that is forever prior to the phenomenal universe is expressing Itself as this whole world play and is in no way separate from It.

I could feel the depth of his realization reverberate in his voice, and his passion for helping others to evolve spiritually was truly awesome. Shankaracharya told me that he is available to seekers 24 hours a day. "That's the Guru's job. It's not a part-time affair," he said with deep humility. As his ashram was under construction, I slept on the floor beneath the Mother's shrine, with the Guru lying just across the room, also on the floor. It was a blissful night, to have such access to this master who literally radiates the light of the supreme Divinity. I felt deeply blessed.

Shankaracharya lives with his spiritual helper, Anandamayi, who receives Devi Bhavas (rare manifestations of the Divine Mother.) They are in a long-term committed relationship which he refers to as yogic. It was beautiful to behold such a pure coming together of two souls both utterly dedicated to serving the Divine. He spoke to me about the beauty of a relationship consecrated to the Divine, where supporting each other in their spiritual expression is the deeper context. He also spoke of relationship as an occasion for love to flash forth, noting that love is already within you, and the relationship is the *occasion* for it to flash forth. Shankaracharya's life embodies the deepest understanding of the eternal unity of Shiva and Shakti.

Meetings With Great Yogis

My first area of enquiry is into your initial contact with the awakened current. Can you tell me about the first stirrings of spiritual desire and the spiritual quest in your own life?

I was working in aerospace engineering in the mid-'60s, which was when the psychedelic revolution and the hippie movement started in the United States. During that time, people were really looking for answers. I started spending time with them and that led me, in 1967, to begin a world-wide search for realized masters. In 1970, this search involved a year-long pilgrimage to India. I hitchhiked. It took a few months going overland to get there. In India, I wandered as a sadhu (renunciate) with no money and lived on temple prasad. Since then, there have been many trips to India.
After spending time with a number of yogis there, I brought back Guru Maharaj, who had just turned 13, to Boulder, Colorado and helped establish his Divine Light Mission in Denver.

In 1974, I went to see Baba Muktananda, who was on tour in the United States. The first day I went for his darshan he said, "You've worked for Guru Maharaj, now you're going to work for me." I thought, *Wow! That's amazing. How would he know that?* I became strongly involved with Baba and eventually ran a center and gave Shaktipat for him. That was between '74 and '77. Coincidentally, it was at Baba's ashram in Ganeshpuri that I first heard about Dhyanyogi and Anandamayi Ma. At that time, I didn't think I'd ever meet either of those beings, who later became major influences in my life.

Later, when I was visiting a friend in California, I heard that Dhyanyogi was up the road at Chico, and we decided to go see him. When we first entered the house, he came out from another room and greeted me, saying, "So, you've come!"

It just so happened, on that particular visit, that he recited the seed sounds of the chakras for the first time in the United States. Each time he would repeat the sound I could feel it inside. It was a very strong experience. Baba Muktananda had a much larger organization, so it was a rare opportunity to be with a being of that magnitude in such a personal and intimate way. I couldn't pass it. I decided to become his disciple.

Years later, while I was living in Westfork, Arkansas, Dhyanyogi came and stayed at my house. Besides being a great blessing, I found it very interesting, because at the last darshan with Baba, in 1977, he gave me a pair of blessed sandals and said, "You'll run a large ashram and take many people across the sea (of samsara.) I'll come and live in it. I'll visit your house." It was the Guru *principle*, coming in a different form. Baba said, "I'll visit your house," and Dhyanyogi came. During his stay, Dhyanyogi performed his once-a-year Navratri anushthan (nine days of austerities) in my meditation closet. Navratri is a time especially sacred to the Shakti. Here was Dhyanyogi, this great Siddha, staying in my bedroom, doing his once-a-year anushthan! And besides that, I was blessed to be able to give him daily massages. It was *really* strong.

After that, Kali started manifesting strongly in my meditations. Dhyanyogi suggested that I come and help him with the establishment of his ashram in Soquel, California. So I moved there. And, when he returned to India, I followed him. It was during that trip that I had the experience I call, "God Alone Is."

How many years was that awakening from the time that you contacted the awakened current?

It was '67 to '81.

God Alone Plays ALL the Roles, There Is Only THAT

What could you say about the progress, or the process, of the awakened Shakti that happened in you during that period of time, between '67 and '81? Why was it so deep and powerful in you that it led to full realization? Certainly that doesn't happen with everyone!

One thing leads to another. A quest for answers led me to Guru Maharaj. That led me to Baba and then to Dhyanyogi. When I went back to India to see Dhyanyogi, I was going to start a 40-day anushthan in Uttarkashi, a time when you go into seclusion and do austerities. The night before it was to start, Anandamayi Ma manifested and said, "Don't start this anushthan. Come and see me."

In a vision she manifested?

Yes, in meditation. So, I went to see Anandamayi Ma at her Kankhal Ashram. I arrived on the first day of the Adi Rudra Fire Yajna, one of her major life events. This yajna was being held for the stability of the earth. I stayed across the street in a small barren room on the Ganga and that evening during meditation had profound experiences with her. The next day when I went to her ashram, there were hundreds of people there. She called me up to wave arati to Her. It was a great honor. When I was waving the light, I felt energy jump from her body into mine. After that, things were stepped up significantly.

After the completion of the Yajna, I remembered a previous suggestion Dhyanyogi had made – to go see Godavari Ma – so I went.

Who was she?

Godavari Ma was a great woman saint who lived in Sakori, which is near Shirdi. On the train ride there, I was so blissed-out and in such an abstracted state, that when the stop was called, I jumped off the train, forgetting my bag and money. The train pulled away and I was left in India with nothing.

Wow!

Everything was stripped away, you might say. Which is when the Divine Mother revealed Herself.

It was when you got off that train, that full awakening happened?

Yes. I was on my way to see Godavari Ma, and everything was stripped away. There was no money. Nothing. Dhyanyogi had had something like a stroke and was very sick – some sort of illness no one could explain. It was after being with Anandamayi Ma, when I was en route to visit Godavari Ma, that I had this experience. The Divine Mother appeared in the forms of the Gurus I had been with – as Baba, as Dhyanyogi, as Anandamayi Ma – and then She appeared in *my* form. Then, she appeared in Her Form, which dissolved into formless Chitti Shakti. There was sparkling Consciousness inside, outside, everywhere. The realization was, *There is only That*. And it was *That* that had been working with me through these great beings, *That* which had appeared as these great beings. There is *only* That. The experience remains unbroken.

Initiation Into Tantra: The Path Of The Mother

Around that time, I was told of a Tantric Guru named Ramesh Moudgil who carries on the Divine Mother tradition. Even though I was having experiences of the Divine Mother and had been with these Kundalini

Gurus, I'd never formally worshipped the Divine Mother and didn't know any of Her sadhanas (spiritual practices.)

You had the realisation of the Mother, before you even...

Prior.

Really? Goodness!

Yes. So, I went to visit Ramesh, took initiation from him, and started Mother sadhanas. He passed many esoteric mantras from the Tantric tradition. It was 1981. I've been with him ever since. While attending a program in Kullu, India, the Shakti jumped from my body into some swamis and they started getting kriyas (yogic movements). They came over and prostrated. That's when it all started.

I went back to Dhyanyogi on Guru Purnima and told him about my experience of the Divine Mother and the Shakti jumping. He said, "You should trust in your realization and take on disciples. You have my blessing." He also blessed the seed sound of the Divine Mother for me to give aspirants.

Dhyanyogi was my meditation guru and Ramesh was my mantra guru. In 2000, Ramesh passed the lineage of the Divine Mother tradition to me, along with a special Guru mantra that was given to him by his Guru.

Wow.

So three things come together here. One is the formal Divine Mother tradition, one is the Shaktipat tradition, and the other is the philosophical, integral teachings that are being presented.

So, you got off the train, and you had that shift in your perception, the recognition that there is only That – that God Alone Is, that it's all the Mother – but you still went on to continue learning?

Yes, to study with Ramesh.

Within That Oneness You Can Still Improve Yourself on a Personal Level

What can you tell me about that? What's the inner experience of someone who has gone beyond duality and is now learning new practices?

Well, you see, from a devotional stance, there's no end to it. As Ramakrishna said, "You can go into a liquor store, have one bottle of liquor, and you're as drunk as you can be. But you're inside a whole liquor store." You walk into the ocean, and anywhere you set your foot in it, you're touching the whole ocean. The Divine Mother is endless, Her Presence is eternal. Everything is Her leela, Her divine play. Naturally, after darshan of the Divine Mother, the feeling arises that you'd like to know more about Her worship.

All of this led to the teaching I'm presenting. It was the vehicle. Philosophically, I'm interested in what the Mother tradition represents. It's an integral philosophy – honoring divinity inherent in life, the importance of living consciously, and the recognition that the Self and the power of the Self are one. It was befitting to learn the traditional worship and mantras associated with a tradition that embodies the Mother, the formal Mother tradition. The Divine Mother passed me a mantra and then later Ramesh gave me the same mantra. This was the mantra that Dhyanyogi later blessed.

So, in a mystical experience, the Divine Mother gave you a mantra?

Yes. It's all connected together. One thing leads to another, which leads to another. It's just the way Consciousness is presenting Itself. It was the formless Mother who appeared *as* the Mother. It was the Mother who sent me to Ramesh, her devotee, to learn more about Her worship and carry on Her tradition. There's no end to self-improvement. Within the idea that *There's only God*, one can still refine oneself.

The experience of Oneness *is* Oneness. However, you might go where there's a lot of meditation and feel a strong presence. Then, you may go somewhere else and not feel the same intensity of presence, all within the same Oneness. Why do great saints go to visit other saints and places of pilgrimage if they've already experienced the Self? Why bother going to a place of pilgrimage? Those are all places where the Self stands revealed. It's natural to go. I mean, if you like pie, then you're going to have a piece of pie. Why not have it?

In the same way that we stopped at the Self-Realization Fellowship today.

Yes.

It's a beautiful place that represents pure consciousness.

Yes, and as you know, God is infinite. And God's glories are infinite. As Ramakrishna said, "Why play only one note on the flute?" It just happens that yogis are drawn to certain things. They're not doing these things to try to get something. It's just natural to be doing them. There's an impulse from within. An attraction.

There's no sense that you're doing it?

There's no sense that you're doing it. There's no sense of need. It's just *what's happening*.

There's no sense of...?

Need. It's just *what's happening*. It's more of a reveling in the bliss of the Self. Take chanting, for example. Before the experience of God, one may do chanting to experience a deeper presence; and after the experience of God, one may still continue to do chanting. But then, it's the glory of the One, reveling within Itself. You know, it's not like, "Well, now I'm going to stop chanting because everything is God. I won't do the mantra anymore, I won't visit saints, I won't learn anything about the Divine Mother or her worship, because I've had darshan of the Divine Mother and realize this is all a play of Consciousness." If you're in a teaching mode, all these things can be especially helpful, because it's a format for people to be able to contact grace – so people can touch that which can't be seen.

The mantra isn't as important as the grace that's being passed through it or where the mantra comes from. *That's* what people touch when they are doing the mantra. The mantra is a vehicle of grace. These traditions are so ancient and the mantras have been used for such a lofty purpose, for so long, that there's a field of energy created by the many saints and practitioners that have gone before. The mantra connects one with that energy, which greatly enhances its effectiveness. When you couple that with the deep philosophy and tremendous blessing of Shaktipat, it all adds up to a very potent circumstance. We can benefit greatly from what's been done for so many years by so many great beings, who have done the same practices and realized God.

Thank you. In my understanding, when a person merges in the Infinite, there's a dissolution of the sense of being separate. And that process of dissolution that happens within the awakening of the spiritual current can often be a frightening experience or can be experienced as a death experience. This is sometimes termed, "the dark night of the soul" or "the dissolution of the self." Did you have this happen in your journey?

There wasn't really a dark night of the soul. For me, the dark night is when you feel fragmented, when you feel separate. And again, I don't teach that "people" reach enlightenment. It is the One that realizes Its own Nature through the vehicle of the person within Its own dream. So it isn't that the *person* wakes up, it's the One that wakes up to Its own true Nature through the vehicle of the person within Its own dream. So there's no sense of attaining anything or being anything special.

So at that moment, at the train station?

When I say the Divine Mother revealed Herself, I mean that Consciousness stood revealed. The nature of one's experience has to do with one's particular approach and belief. My own belief was that the one God was helping me through these various saints.

And so it happened that the Divine Mother appeared in the forms of the saints I had been close to, and then in my form, which showed that the same One that appeared as the saints was appearing as me. And then, she appeared in her formless nature, which is Brahman or Shiva-Shakti, which is everything. It's like the water in the waves. And that's what I teach. You know, this is the Mother's dance, the power of the Self. All these forms are manifestations of That. And That's inherent in all these forms. So I teach things that support that Experience, that perpetuate unity Awareness – that it's the One appearing in *all* these guises.

But just because the One appears in many guises, doesn't mean there's not a distinct advantage in being one-pointed in your approach. When I was with Baba, I was one-pointed on Baba and worshipped him as the Guru. And that led to Dhyanyogi. Then, I was totally fixed on Dhyanyogi and started having visions of the Divine Mother!

When I was a disciple of Dhyanyogi, Anandamayi Ma appeared in meditation and said, "Come and see me." So I went to visit her, and what happened, happened. After that, the Divine Mother showed me that it was She who was appearing in all these guises. They were all part of the grace-bestowing Power – the fifth aspect of Shakti – the Self-revealing aspect. It was the same Guru, the One World Teacher. In fact, when I met Dhyanyogi, he said to me, "Baba and I appear as two on the surface, but underneath, we're one." And that was a nice thing to hear.

Integration – Diversity Is Contained Within the Reality of Unity

People often speak about a period of integration after the shift into a non-dual awareness. Did you experience anything like that, where your body and mind needed to readjust to that new consciousness?

In This Reality, the formless and form are one. And diversity is inside of the reality of Unity. It's like one thing expands into another. The broader Reality includes the other reality within It. It isn't so much that individuality is lost, but that the Reality of universality is gained. And then, the universal Reality expresses Itself through the personality.

So there wasn't a sense of disorientation. There was always a sense of *more* orientation. In other words, one reality expanded into another that already contained the more contracted reality within it, as it kept expanding. It wasn't threatening because, by nature, I am interested in whatever – bring it on! The thing is, I wanted to surrender, I wanted to expand, I wanted to experience more. For me it was a thrilling process.

Many saints say, "You're asleep. Wake up!" What does that mean? We're not asleep. I see you, and we're talking. What they mean is, there's another Reality that this waking state is inside of. In normal waking awareness you can remember the dream state, but when you're dreaming you might not be aware of the waking state. That's why we call *this* the waking reality. However, this waking reality is within another expanded Reality. It is movements in that supreme Awareness with inherent identifications that give rise to the waking reality of physical beings and objects. Supreme Awareness is the Waking Reality from this waking state.

The real waking up?

Well, you could say that. However, I wouldn't say that any of it is *unreal*. It's *all* real.

Because it's all the Self.

It's all the Self. As Anandamayi Ma used to say, "Where is there ascent and descent, if there's only the One?" But, yes, from a relative sense, it could be looked at that way.

The Value Of Darshan

So you had an intense focus on awakening through your period of sadhana. You were saying that you lived in seclusion and did extensive practices?

Like many, I was looking for answers. I wanted to deepen my understanding of life – of what's going on. I grew up in the '50s, graduated from high school in '61, and there wasn't a lot available at that time. Not much in the bookstores, not many spiritual masters running around in the United States. But in the mid-'60s, the psychedelic revolution brought a big shift as people started looking for answers and experimenting with other realities. It seemed natural to go to India to look for masters and try to bring them back to the U.S. My nature was to find people I felt had attained something. I wanted to spend time with them so I could attain something too. I was always orientated that way, more than towards books. I was orientated around grace and the value of being with people who were in expanded states. The idea was that, by spending time with them, something would rub off and things would open up.

So you intuited that possibility back then?

I was always attracted to being in the energy of people who had experienced more of what I was trying to get into.

So now, given that this awakening has happened, as you say, not to you but through you, and this capacity to function as a guru, a teacher, a vessel of grace, is active in you – what is your understanding of the way that this process works? What have you got to say about that? The fact that when someone sits with you, this awareness is contagious in a way?

What else would be happening?

I intend this book to be not only for people who are familiar with what were talking about, but also, I hope, for a lot of people who have never heard of this.

Well, it's only natural that you feel, to a certain degree, the experience or state of any person you're with. You know, if you're with someone who's angry, you feel anger. If you're with someone who's experiencing Shakti, then *that* experience is keyed off in you. It's natural that a person is influenced by the aura or the energy they're around. There's a book titled, *The Hidden Messages in Water,* that shows how different sounds and intentions affect water. Water was frozen after being exposed to various vibrations, and then the crystalline structures were photographed. Uplifting feelings gave rise to beautiful patterns. A good percentage of our body is water. So, if you're spending time with people in altered states, or deeper absorption, it tends to draw you into a similar experience. That's a lot more valuable than just reading about these things — it's the *living* reality. It's not just intellectual. It's tangible and it's felt.

That's the value of holy places. That's the value of darshan and satsang. Satsang isn't just *words* of truth; it's the *company* of Truth. True satsang comes from a state of expanded awareness and the words are vehicles through which you actually touch something beyond the words. Someone could speak just one word that might affect you very deeply, whereas someone else could talk for hours with little effect. The words are vehicles to touch something deeper — the actual experience of those speaking.

That's why we play the tapes of these saints. It's not because they have the best sounding voices, it's because they're in That state. You're touching That by association with their pictures, their teaching, their words, their chanting, whatever. It's the power of association. And what can be a greater association than to be with people who have given their life to the supreme quest, people who are in expanded states of awareness? Obviously, that's going to be more productive than being with skeptics, people who don't believe there's anything divine inside. Baba Muktananda used to say that a large part of the spiritual path is the power of company — what we keep company with in the mind.

There's no question that, for me, the greatest blessing was to have spent time with these great saints. It's through their blessing that whatever has been able to happen has happened.

Thank you. That's very beautiful.

It's actually the One that appears in the guise of the saint, blesses Itself in the guise of the aspirant, and then reveals Itself to Itself, within Itself. It plays *all* the roles. *That's* all there is. There's nothing other than That. We worship the Divine Mother because She's the Power of the Self, the reflective Power of Consciousness that makes it possible for the circle to be complete. The One experiences Itself in Its own creation.

First, there's a sense of separation, fragmentation, individuality, and diversity. Then, the One stands revealed in the midst of that diversity. The One sees Itself within Itself and the circle is complete.

Consciousness Awakens To Itself: There Are No Enlightened People

You draw a distinction between the experience of an aspirant, when there's a fluctuation between the ecstasy of God and the turmoil of the world, and enlightenment, where it doesn't matter what state you're in, because there's a recognition that all states are the Mother, or the Divine, or the Self.

That's true. However, it's hard to talk about enlightenment because everyone has their own idea about what that means. I just say, "God Alone Is." It means, *There is only That*. The awareness that *There is only That*, stands revealed. In other words, the universe has been absorbed back into the Self. It's not that the Self is something *other* than the universe. One may negate the universe to turn within, but then this universe must be absorbed back into the Self, so there is *only* the Self. We call *that* enlightenment. It's not that someone *attains* enlightenment. It's not that there's a sense of attainment.

Can you go more deeply into that? You say there are no enlightened people?

No enlightened people. You might say that life is a dream in supreme Awareness. Or, if you think of God in the personal sense, that this is God's dream. All phenomena are movements in supreme Awareness with inherent identifications. And a person is a movement in the dream of the Dreamer. It's the Dreamer that wakes up to Its own Nature through the vehicle of a person within Its own dream. Supreme Consciousness rests in Its own true Nature. There's a reflective quality in an individual – one can reflect on one's true Nature. That's what we call "vimarsha" – the reflective quality of consciousness. So what happens is that the One reflects on Its own Nature and realizes Itself through the vehicle of a person within Its own dream. It isn't that the *person* realized anything, the Dreamer did. It's Consciousness that's appearing in the *guise* of the person; it's Consciousness that realises its own true Nature. That's why I say, *people* don't reach enlightenment – the *One* realizes Its own true Nature within Itself.

Would you say you wake up from the person as consciousness?

The One wakes up to Its own true Nature through the vehicle of a person within Its own dream.

And the inherent identifications?

If you dream Jack and, in your dream, Jack reaches enlightenment, then you're *dreaming* Jack reaching enlightenment. *You're* the dreamer that Jack is *in*. You see what I mean? It's supreme Consciousness that's appearing in the guise of the particular individual. And it's supreme Consciousness that realizes Its own true Nature. There's nothing *other* than That. Ultimately, there's no such thing as people. It all depends on how you look at it. There is and there isn't. It's paradoxical.

Would you say there appears to be?

There appears to be. From a certain angle, you could say there is, and from another angle, you could say – if people imply separate individuals – then, ultimately, there's only the One playing all the roles. You see?

Inherent in the depth of that realization is the recognition, or the realization, that nothing's ever happened. This world has never existed. There's only ever been what Is. And at the same time — simultaneously, you might say — this world of change exists?

It's paradoxical. Both things are true. That's the beautiful thing. You can say the world exists and you can also say it doesn't, and *both* things are true. The world exists if you look at it as being Consciousness appearing as all these guises. The world doesn't exist if you look at it as being something *other* than Consciousness. It just depends on how you view it — the world is as you see it. If you see all this as Consciousness, then you can say the world exists.

That's not an awareness that a person has?

Well, again, it's paradoxical. When you take something back to its source, the source of that experience is not a person; the source of the experience is Consciousness. Consciousness reveals Itself within Itself, through the guise of an individual within Its own manifestation. So the source is Consciousness. It's Consciousness that wakes up, through the vehicle of the person, to Its own true Nature.

So I prefer to say it's Consciousness that's the end revealer. Because a person is a gradation of Awareness — a movement in Awareness with inherent identifications that give rise to the sense of being an individual. It's good to talk in reference to the roots. We have to think, *Really, what is a person?*

What is a person?

What is the sense of perception that we have? Why do we even have perception? Is there even anything *outside?* Is there even any such thing as a world? Or people in it?

And what do you say?

There's *only* Consciousness. There are infinite realities and infinite planes. And, in the nature of Consciousness, anything is possible. There are worlds within worlds, realms within realms. There's a story in which Leela, the yogini, was meditating on the goddess, Saraswati. The goddess appeared and showed her that she was married to two husbands simultaneously, each living with her in a different reality, because at the time of death, the last thought in each of their minds was to be with her. So they both found themselves incarnate in realities where they were each married to her. These are all interesting possibilities. As I said, the possibilities in Consciousness are truly infinite.

Reincarnation has to do with reincarnation of *states*, not just specific places, like, *This is Earth, and this is where we all reincarnate.* Earth, too, is an inherent identification in Consciousness.

The Earth is an identification in consciousness?

Yes. These are all movements in Awareness with inherent identifications that give rise to physical-ness. For example, your waking state may be mirrored in the dream state, where you don't walk through walls and you don't pass through closed doors, because you're programmed in the waking state to believe that those things can't happen. But sometimes, in the dream reality, you find yourself levitating, flying, doing all sorts of things. It's just programming. People can enter the subtle body and do all kinds of things. If they can shed the programming, they can move outside the body and visit saints, go to different lokas (planes) and get teachings – all kinds of possibilities when they're in the subtle body.

There are infinite realities, but the main thing is: what is it that's appearing in *all* these guises? We can spend our whole life arguing and debating over the different planes and different realities and different philosophies and who's higher – that is, which is the "greatest" manifestation? – who is the "real" Kalki Avatar, and so on. But what it all boils down to is: what is the nature of Consciousness Itself, getting absorbed in the eternal Presence, living consciously, and seeing the ego in the context of Reality. There are infinite possibilities in the nature of Consciousness.

Just seeing infinite possibilities in the nature of consciousness frees you up from having a fixed perspective that things are a certain way, that consciousness is fixed.

Yes, and to see it that way would limit Consciousness, because we need only to look around at the different saints and different traditions to see that there *are* many ways and many manifestations.

From Ramana Maharshi and Anandamayi Ma, to Ramakrishna?

Yes, so many! Some of the Gurus are married; some are single. Some are celibate; some are not. Some worship Vishnu, some worship the formless, some do this, and some do that. There are so many saints, so many flavors, so many traditions. It becomes apparent that the One manifests in many ways. So why wouldn't we look at it that way? Why would we look at it in ways that don't reflect the nature of what Reality is? Why not allow Shakti to be infinite and just be in the awe and wonder of Its infinity, instead of thinking we're in a position to judge Shakti? Our job is to *surrender* to God, not to barter with or judge God.

Not to barter?

Yes. Like, *I did this, and now I expect things to go the way I want, otherwise, I won't believe in You*. Of course, Reality stands whether one believes or not. Our job is not to judge God, but to surrender to God – God, meaning that Shiva and Shakti are one. The reflective quality of Awareness gives rise to the sense of "I AM," which is what we call God. Supreme Awareness is aware of Its own existence, so it has Beingness. The Power of the Self *is* that reflective Awareness. The first movement in supreme Awareness is the awareness that *I exist, I AM*. It's the Power of the Self and *everything* springs from That.

So once awareness becomes aware of itself, then manifestation arises?

It's not that it *becomes* aware of itself – it *is* aware of itself. Being is beyond becoming.

So when you say that's the first movement, it's also the eternal movement?

The eternal. Yes. When I say *first* movement, I mean from this normal waking reality, looking in that direction. But it's actually beyond time and the sense of "first." It's the eternal Awareness of the One revelling in Its own Nature.

It's The Shakti That's Giving Shaktipat

So my question is, when and how did the Shakti flower within you to the point where you could give Shaktipat?

Well, the Shaktipat traditions were something I was really drawn to because they seemed to have such a transformative quality. The power was working so strongly that it would produce spontaneous yogas from the inside out. There's a power inherent in many traditions – a subtle power at work. However, when that power is working so strongly that it gives rise to spontaneous yogic processes such as asana, pranayama, bandha, etc., then we call it the Shaktipat tradition.

The difference is that you're not the doer, you're *being done*. When you're practicing things – even when it's a worthwhile practice – ultimately, it's still producing karma, because *you're* doing it. In Shaktipat, the divine Power Itself is doing you. And whatever is necessary, takes place. In Shaktipat, the awakened Kundalini is purifying the psyche and reducing the karmic load. Shaktipat is an extraordinary blessing.

When you give Shaktipat?

I don't *give* it; it just *happens*.

It happens? So, in your world, it's just all consciousness, and one of the things that happens to happen around you is the Shaktipat?

It's the Shakti. It's the Shakti that's giving Shaktipat. It's the Shakti that's approaching Itself and revealing Itself, within Itself. My awareness is that the people who are approaching me are approaching the Mother through me, and the Mother is giving Her response. There's no sense of doing anything. There's no sense of being anything. It's just what's happening.

Could you also say that there's a sense that you're doing everything and being everything?

I don't look at it that way, but there could be that sense.

Okay.

Seeing The Ego In The Context Of Reality

Because, even though the personality exists within a much broader awareness, it's still dangerous for the personality to assert itself in an egoistic way.

Certain things can reinforce the ego's stance of separateness and the sense that *I'm doing something. I'm giving something. I've attained something.* When a jnani talks that way, he's speaking of the "I" as something beyond the ego, or personality. However, I prefer not to water the ego by looking at it that way. Because, this is all the Mother's leela, and maya has touched even the greatest of saints.

It's in the stories of the Puranas. Ramakrishna used to pray, "Oh Mother, please keep your maya far away from me." Even though he was an avatar, he didn't ever think, *I'm above maya; nothing can touch me.* He was always in the stance of the devotee, which is a safe stance, no matter what your experience. The stance of the devotee does not represent separateness if you're aware that it's the One that's appearing as the devotee and being devoted to Itself. This doesn't give water to the ego/personality. When Consciousness identifies with being an ego, It becomes limited. When Consciousness turns back on Its own true Nature and expresses Itself through the ego, *that's* another story. Then the ego is seen in the context of Reality and it can't hurt you.

So, when the ego is being seen in the context of reality, how is the ego seen?

One can see through it and see that's it's a guise. It's an expression of Awareness but it doesn't *limit* Awareness. In other words, That, which is free and beyond the ego, can use the ego as a vehicle to express Itself. The ego is simply a vehicle. It's an entirely different matter when awareness is identified with being an ego, than when it turns back on its own true Nature and expresses Itself *through* the ego. There's a big difference.

That's what I call *seeing the ego in the context of Reality.*

And I'm of the school of thought that believes that people can reach self-realization and still have certain things they haven't refined in their personality.

Yeah.

Because, in many traditions, personal development is not a focus. In fact, very little emphasis may be placed on the validity of the world, the basic idea being to turn within and detach yourself. Refinement of the personality might not be part of the process. Then, if one experiences the Self, their experience may be expressed through an *unrefined* personality. Whereas if part of your process, along with meditation, is to develop purity of intention, divine love, compassion, surrender, divine ignorance, etc., and then you experience the Self, then that will be expressed through a *refined* personality. This can be very beneficial, especially if other people are approaching you for guidance.

There's no doubt that our engagement with life can be part of the path of recognition and transformation. And I feel that, along with the inner processes, a *conscious* engagement is essential, especially in this culture. It helps bring forth the possibility that, as one does sadhanas and experiences expanded awareness, something great can be done to help bring about a better world, instead of creating more yogi demons. Yogi demons, like Ravana and Mahishasura, did the same mantras the saints did. They worshipped God, but they had self-centered motives.

The Ego Of Knowledge And The Ego Of Doership

You know, from an absolute sense, nobody really knows anything. For instance, you go for a job – *I want that job!* – but maybe if you didn't get that job, a better job would come along. Or maybe you'd get raped on the job. So the idea is, since you need the job, you go for the job, but the intention is: *Whatever is best spiritually, let that come to pass.* You do what *seems* best, with the awareness of allowing what is best to occur. It's the ego of knowledge and the ego of doership that keep one in bondage.

The ego of knowledge and the ego of doership — can you elaborate?

Both have to be decimated.

Decimated?

Say you go to heal somebody. Maybe if you *didn't* heal that person, they'd reach up for God. So, by healing them, you've actually prevented their reaching towards God. You go to heal them, saying, "I want this person to be healed," as if you know what's best. It's better to go help someone because they need help, with the intention of *Whatever's best spiritually, let that come to pass.* That intention takes the ego of knowledge out. In order to know anything, you'd have to know everything.

Can you elaborate?

You'd have to know the past, present, and future of every being. Someone might get AIDS and, because of having AIDS, they'd wake up and become more compassionate — but you're not going to wish that someone would have AIDS. Or maybe your wife might leave you and, because of that, you find something within yourself and become a greater being — but you're not going to wish your wife would leave.

In the spiritual realm, whatever brings transformation carries grace — whatever guise it comes in. And often, what we know, or what we want, or what we think, is not necessarily what will bring awakening. From the spiritual standpoint, the self-revealing process is the summum bonum of what's going on. Whatever's happening, if it brings transformation, then grace is at work, whether or not from your perspective it's desirable or undesirable. Adopt the disposition: *Whatever's best spiritually, let that come to pass.*

Well, what would we use as a guiding principle?

It's the intention that's a guiding principle.

The Intention being?

Whatever's best spiritually, let that come to pass.

Isn't that still going to bring into play ideas from our conditioning and culture?

You're trying to do what *seems* best, but not with the absolute sense that you *know* what's best.

Oh, Okay. So, I'll do what seems best…

It's your intention.

Acknowledging that I really don't know. It seems best that I offer you a cup of tea although I don't really know – maybe you're allergic to tea.

It's the intention. In other words, you respond to situations in life as they present themselves with what *seems* to be appropriate. The ego of knowledge comes from the position that you *know* what's best from an absolute standpoint. But you really don't. Maybe someone will go on a spiritual retreat and the retreat center will burn down, and they'll get disillusioned with God and leave the spiritual path. Maybe someone will go to a house of prostitution and discover, *I really want to go deeper than what's here. This isn't going to give me what I'm looking for.* We can't say. I wouldn't recommend the house of prostitution. I'd say, "Here, try these spiritual practices. They've helped a lot of people." The human mind is the human mind. It makes suggestions but it doesn't know definitely what is best. You see, in my teaching, it's not the specifics that matter so much; it's how one looks at the specifics. I'm always turning people back to *how* they're looking at things, not what they're looking at. Do you understand?

Yeah, I do.

It doesn't matter to me so much *what* one is looking at – it's *how* they're looking, how they're affected by it. It's whether it has transformative value. Not what the situation is.

Yeah.

I place very little emphasis on, *You should do this; you should do that. You shouldn't do this; you shouldn't do that.* It's more, *How do you look at it and how does it affect you?*

How do you relate to it?

Yes, how do you relate to it, and to consider, *Why am I saying what I'm saying? What am I really serving?* It's the purity of intention behind what's being said that really tells the story, and what would be a greater service than to see God in others and to invoke God's Presence there? In the same way that everyone has a point of awareness within them, and we turn within to go back to our source, that same point of awareness exists in everything "outside" and we can also honor and serve it there. Whether we turn our attention within or without, we can still court the same Reality.

The nature of Shakti is fluid. It's universal. We should look at things in ways that support That. And one way to do so is to see the ego for what it is – to see it in the context of Reality. That's supportive of awakening *and* supportive of a better world.

Yeah.

Then that ego becomes a beautiful vessel for that experience to express itself.

Could we relate this to the Buddhist notions of developing love and kindness and compassion?

Yes. And that brings to mind an important thing. Sometimes people talk about what's higher, the Heart or the Sahasrar. It's one thing, being in the experience of the Heart on the way up to the Sahasrar, and it's another thing, being in the experience of the Heart on the way down. On the way up, you have love and compassion for all beings, but you experience them as being separate from yourself.

Conscious Embrace

After the realization of the universal Self in Sahasrar, when Kundalini descends to the heart and expresses Itself as compassion, there is no longer a sense of dualism. When the realisation of Sahasrar is brought to the heart, the whole world is then seen as God, and the realisation is made manifest.

So you're saying that it's more holistic in a sense to bring the understanding of unity into the world and therefore serve the Self in everything and everyone you see, rather than to just simply seek to merge yourself exclusively into a Divine domain that may or may not have a beneficial effect on the way you relate to others.

Well, there are different times and different circumstances. What we find now – which is part of the evolution of what's happening in the world – is that many people are engaged in relationships, working, living in the world and, at the same time, becoming more interested in Self-awareness and Self-realization. Obviously, a lot of their energy is spent going outward. It's not that we're living like Ramana Maharshi, Shankaracharya, or someone who lived a hundred years ago, like Ramakrishna. This is a different time and a different place. Back then people didn't have multiple relationships. They didn't have girlfriends. Women weren't out in the workplace – people weren't living this way. Basically, they lived in a different reality.

In the reality that we find ourselves in now, it's very important that we have our inner life, but it's also very important that the outer *becomes* the inner, by serving the same reality there. Through conscious engagement, life can be transformative, and the world can benefit, as well. It's essential and it's what's needed in this current paradigm in the West. To have the inner life and to also live consciously, embracing situations and serving the One in those situations, is the Tantric path of embrace.

Can you tell me more about that?

To embrace life consciously, one does not see everything in life as an obstacle. Rather, one sees the Divine inherent in *everything*. Say you follow the path of detachment and, ultimately, consider the world to be an illusion. If you have a girl friend, then it's likely that you'd look upon her as an obscuration of the inner Self. Then you say, "Let's have sex." She's seen as an obscuration, but you want to have sex with her. It doesn't add up! The other way of looking at her is as a manifestation of the Divine Mother. You can see her as an obscuration or you can see her as a manifestation of the Divine. If you look at her as a manifestation of the Divine Mother and invoke the Divine Mother in her, that brings forth the

Divine Mother's presence. Because, wherever God is worshipped, God's presence comes forth. If you just think she's an obstacle, that's not the approach of conscious embrace. That's the approach of detachment and negation.

Ah ha.

That approach works well for renunciates and people who are disassociating from the body and the world, who go into seclusion and turn within. It doesn't work well for people in this culture who are engaged in life. There's more to the world than it just being an obscuration of reality. The world *springs* from the Divine, and it's possible that the Divine can stand revealed *in* this reality. That possibility exists, and we can be part of the process if we choose to honor it. So, why not? As long as we're here, why not?

Thank you.

The Earth Is An Inherent Identification In Consciousness

One thing that I've been asking each of the teachers in the interviews for this book is about our relationship with the Earth. We see all around us destruction, degradation, global warming, people living life at a faster and faster pace. How and where does God consciousness fit in? What is your attitude toward this current world situation?

The world is made up of people, so the greatest help for the world is to have more people living in the world who live consciously. Obviously, life moves as it moves and certain situations give rise to other situations. There are many beliefs and there's a lot of hatred. We're not all separate in this world; we're all part of the overall movement. Even though what you may be doing may seem like a small part, rest assured, your thoughts and deeds have some impact, no matter how slight, on all sentient beings.

The other thing to consider is that there are infinite realities and infinite planes. Of course, we do what we can to make this world a better place, as it's our karma to be incarnated into this situation at this time. There are more desirable realities that exist in the now. Siddha Loka exists now. Infinite realms exist now. It's just that we find our consciousness identified at this time with this reality and this circumstance. Our job is to live consciously, and serving others is part of that.

We should also realise that whatever's happening in the world is perfect, and even though we work to remove suffering, we must see the perfection in suffering. Situations in life don't come about from nowhere. There are many influences that gave rise to each particular situation and each situation has its own effects, which mix with the effects of other situations. In reality, the entire movement of life is involved in each situation. What we do carries on. It's tremendously important that we serve and live the highest ideals.

The movement of life yields exactly what it yields. There is a supreme Intelligence that all unintelligent acts take place in that deems that they yield exactly what they yield. And if we are not seeing that perfection in apparent imperfection, then we have more to attain within ourselves.

There's more to attain?

There's more to attain until one sees perfection in imperfection. Even though one's working to remove suffering, one must see the perfection in suffering – and honor it.

The Whole Universe Is Involved Right Here, Right Now

You've said that doership and knowledge are what create the illusion that consciousness is limited, and also you were saying earlier that the human being is really a conglomerate of –

Influences.

Influences, not in reality a separate person, but really – all of our actions are part of the vaster, larger, overall movement of life.

Life is expressing itself. The movement of life is expressing itself in a unique way as an individual. The stream produces the current. The stream is the movement of life, the current is the individual. The movement of life is nothing more than movements within awareness with inherent identifications – that's what the movement of life is. Everyone you've met, everyone your parents met, are all part of what's given rise to who you think you are. There's nothing in this world that, to some degree, at some level, has not affected the experience of who you are right now. You're a unique expression of life – a face of life.

A face?

A face of life. An expression of this movement of life.

You also say that it's all happening in Supreme Intelligence. So can we assume that Supreme Intelligence is what's giving rise to the totality of the movement of life?

It all springs from supreme Intelligence. Often we can see supreme Intelligence peeking through these various situations.

How so?

You can see it in the order in the universe. You can see it in nature, in healing processes. You can see it in various ways where Consciousness stands revealed, where there's more awareness.

Kundalini, grace, higher states of consciousness glimpsed?

Yes. When supreme Consciousness is so absorbed in Its own effulgence that It forgets Itself as the source of the effulgence, the incipiencies of dualism occur. That ultimately gives rise to the sense of "I" and "this," where the "this" is seen as separate from the "I." The fact is that all appearances take place *within* supreme Awareness and supreme Awareness is *inherent* in all these appearances. Even in pain, even in stones. Supreme Awareness is inherent in everything because everything is a modification of It. In some manifestations, Consciousness stands revealed and, in others, consciousness stands concealed. In humans, there's a reflective quality, whereas in a tree or rock, this may not be the case. But they're all still essentially Consciousness. And part of the nature of this Awareness is that movements within it yield exactly what they yield.

Can you elaborate?

Yes, for instance, whatever I'm saying now, the effects of it will yield exactly what it yields. Whatever you're doing is mixing together with what I'm doing, and the combination will yield what it yields. Anandamayi is in the other room doing what she's doing and that touches us. And it goes out. I mean, maybe you know Master Charles, or you know someone else, so that connection with them in some way connects them with what you're doing here. And I'm connected with you, so they're involved with me, too. Everything's involved. The whole universe is involved. Right here, right now. And life's moving as it moves. And that's what's happening.

All situations have given rise to this circumstance. And these situations will give rise to the next circumstance. That circumstance is not coming from nowhere. The movement of life has given rise to it. And inherent in all these situations is that supreme Intelligence. Self-recognition starts happening when awareness turns back on its own roots, its true Nature, in the midst of this karmic field.

There Is Only THE Power – It's Not YOUR Power

Understanding that we're being done – like characters in a dream, that we're being dreamed – and that we're being lived – in what sense is it spiritually beneficial to deepen that understanding?

To realize that you're being done?

Yes.

Well, there are two ways of looking it. Let's say the baby's hungry and you're a woman with breasts, so you feed the baby. This can be viewed in the ego sense: *Look, how great I am, I'm feeding the baby with my nutritious milk!* Or, the awareness could be: *The movement of life has given rise to me, my breasts and my baby. Now life's feeding the baby through me.* In both views, the baby is still getting fed, except in one case, there's the ego doership, and in the other case, there isn't.

I see.

And the ego of doership supports the idea of your being separate. Of being the doer. Of being the one who's in control of everything.

There's no such thing as "personal" power. There's only *The Power*. It's not *your* power. *You're in It.*

You're IN IT. You're IN THE POWER. It's not your power; you're an instrument of the power.

It's not *your* Power. You're *in The Power.*

Or an expression of The Power.

Yes. People are on a quest for personal power, but the greatest personal power is to surrender to *The Power* and realize that you exist because of *It*. It's not that *The Power* exists because of you as an individual or ego entity. It's *The Power*. When you surrender to *The Power*, then all of a sudden, there's tremendous power manifesting around you.

Because you're invoking the Presence, which is where the real power is.

Yes.

So that's a major element – it seems like a beautiful element of your teaching.

Yes. Externally, it's still going to look like you're doing the same things as everyone else – you're talking with someone; you're doing what you can do to help out. But inside, there's something else going on. The way you see things – your orientation – is different. And this allows something else to occur. Because when you think it's *your* power, then you're operating with *your* power. When you realize it's *The Power* and you're in *It*, then all of a sudden, *That* starts operating.

So coming into the disposition that you're in The Power and that's what's operating, part of having that awareness is that it affects the way The Power operates – is what you just said?

Yes, because we superimpose our own belief, our own way of looking at things, *on* The Power, and that affects how The Power manifests *through* us. That's why so many teachings have so many jingles.

Because of their different attitudes toward consciousness.

Different attitudes.

So, it's paradoxical then?

It's paradoxical.

It's also saying that the attitude of the ego will affect the way the power functions – very paradoxical, because the less the ego attributes the power to itself, the more power will come into play.

That's true.

That's a real and very cool paradox. It seems like a very nice complement to the idea of refining the ego. That's kind of coming clearer for me.

Seeing the ego in the context of reality. I mean, the self-centred ego is one thing and the selfless ego is quite another. The ego is the characteristic of awareness that assimilates things and makes them one's own. Like, *I lived here, I had these parents.* These are ego characteristics. The saints can tell you who their parents were and where they lived. And they may have their preferences – maybe they won't wear a red shirt, or eat a certain way, or this or that. However, that doesn't hurt them because they see things in the context of Reality. When Consciousness is identified with being an ego, that's different than when Consciousness turns back on Its own true Nature and then expresses Itself through the ego. Personal preferences just float on the periphery of that Reality.

They float?

They don't limit reality. Reality expresses Itself through you. Whether you have short hair, long hair, a shaved head, or a Mohawk is insignificant. Reality still stands. However, if the consciousness in you is identified with just being a person who looks and acts a certain way, then that gives rise to a different experience of reality.

Practicing Witness Awareness

You said that the worst type of ego is the ego that tries to usurp the power of God and thinks that it is the subject? That seems like a danger there.

That's the pitfall in the Advaitic path – especially for people in the western circumstance who have girlfriends, jobs, and everything else. It's a great misunderstanding to find a place in the mind that witnesses other things in the mind, and then consider that place in the mind to be supreme Witness Awareness! Really, all it is, is the ego witnessing its own movements. It's just a place in the mind that's witnessing the other things going on in the mind. It's not The Witness that's witnessing *all* minds. The difference between The Witness and a place in the mind that's mimicking witness awareness, is that the place in the mind that's mimicking witnesses awareness is just seeing things through the sense organs. The Witness is seeing things from the universal Reality and witnessing through *all* sensory organs. You know what I mean? It's universal.

The grandest ego trip is for the ego to take on the guise of illumination, proclaiming, *I am the Self. Why should I do a practice? Why should I do a mantra? Why should I be with a Guru? I have everything inside.* Then, to top it off, that ego may even start proclaiming its own glory in the guise of being a spiritual teacher. This is maya to the nth degree. God is omniscient and omnipotent.

It's very easy to just read a book and then, all of a sudden, take the disposition of witness awareness and think you've attained everything. But *real* Witness Awareness doesn't happen just in the conscious mind; it has to do with the subconscious. It has to do with the superconscious. The witness awareness that one practices in the conscious mind has to progress through the whole psyche, so that the entire psyche is purified. It's not just that, all of a sudden you're thinking, *I'm just going to sit back and witness things.*

True Witness Awareness permeates all realities and is not limited to your sense perceptions.

Is witness awareness in that sense the same as universal presence, or presence?

Well, I don't really talk about witness awareness as being the main objective, anyway. It's a technique. It's a practice. To mimic Witness Awareness means to find a place where you can step back from melodrama and look at things without being so affected. But it's not meant to be used to reinforce the ego sense of *Look at how great I am!* Or, *I understand this.* Or, *I'm God.* Anyway, why can't we practice witness awareness without a sense of negation, without thinking, *I'm not this, not this – neti, neti?*

Can you elaborate? I don't quite understand.

Well, many practicing witness awareness take the stance, *I'm not the body, I'm not the mind, I'm not the world,* in order to go back to the Source. But why not just witness things without the connotation, *I'm not this?* Because, ultimately, it's the One that's appearing as all this anyway.

So, you're saying, "Look at all this," without having any idea about it?

Well, just practice witness awareness without the connotation that *I'm not this.*

Courting The Kundalini – We Owe Our Existence To That Great Power

Okay. You speak about Kundalini courtship – could you elaborate on that idea? Richard Moss also speaks about"Courting the Life Force" and I wonder if it's something similar?

Well, we owe our existence to that great Power and whatever experience we may have is due to It. If you practice the path of Jnana, whatever your experience may be, it falls within the realm of Shakti. So to court It, to develop a personal relationship with this divine Power – even if it is formless – we start embracing ideas that are supportive of its nature. And we honor it within ourselves and within others. Just like courting a woman, if we do things to win her over, she embraces us. So, too, if we surrender and serve the Shakti through thought, word, and deed, then we become more and more absorbed in the Shakti, and It expresses Itself in more expansive ways through us.

Living with reverence, living in a way that fosters devotion.

Yes. To court the Shakti means to honor the Shakti. If you negate the Shakti – if you have a girlfriend and see her as an obscuration of some kind – you're not honoring that the Shakti is manifesting in the guise of the girlfriend. Maybe there's something to learn there. Maybe there's something to serve there. Maybe you can court the Divine through this situation – or any situation. Honoring the Shakti isn't just honoring the Shakti in the temple or in meditation, it's also honoring the Shakti consciously in how we engage with life.

And that's where people run into the problem, because the only thing they see is suffering and delusion and ignorance, and it's hard for them to honor the Shakti in the midst of all that. In India, they can take a stone and worship the Mother there, and then people start experiencing miracles around that stone because the Presence has been invoked. If the Presence can be invoked in a stone image, then you can also invoke the Presence in your wife. You can invoke the Presence anywhere.

It just depends on how you look at it. You might go to Rishikesh and there might be 350 ashrams there, each one with a Guru. Some of these Gurus may not necessarily be in exalted states; however, because they're Gurus and others look at them with reverence, that invokes the Presence, and people start having divine experiences around them. There are two things going on: there's the person's way of looking at things that invokes the Presence, and there can also be something coming from what they're looking at. Now, if they're looking at something that there's nothing coming from, they can *still* invoke the Presence there. You can look at the statue of the Divine Mother with reverence and that draws forth the divine Presence there. Then, anyone in that arena can benefit from those subtle vibrations. However, if the image has never been worshipped and you don't look at it with reverence, then it's a dead deal. A really good situation is when you look at the Guru in the right way *and* the Guru is in an expanded reality and is looking at you in a favourable way. Then *both* things are happening.

Both viewing each other as Divine?

Yes, and the true Guru doesn't see anyone as an "other" – it's all just the One. They see the *One* approaching the *One*. The Mother is appearing in their guise to reveal Herself, and the Mother is appearing in the guise of the seeker, and then the Mother is experiencing Herself within Her own Self. So they would see it all as The Mother. They may even bow down to the person coming to them for knowledge – they're honouring the Mother. They don't have a sense of otherness, you know?

The Sense Of "Who You Are" Is The Cloth Of The Mother

In one of the little aphorisms on the Mother in your book, "God Alone Is," you said, "Who is left to perceive her?"

She stands alone.

So, what can you say about that? It strikes me as the most poignant point in all of this, and that is: who is left standing?

Well, that's the thing. You might say the Mother covers her nakedness with all of these realities. The Mother's inner nature is Brahman, which She covers with all Her phenomena.

Ah ha.

You cannot see the Mother in Her nakedness because you're part of the phenomena. So when the cloth of the Mother is removed – the sense of who you are is "the cloth of the Mother" – then there's no one left to perceive Her in Her nakedness except Herself. She stands alone. The Awareness that's left is the Awareness of the Mother Herself – not fragmented awareness that gives rise to a sense of being someone separate who's perceiving Her. The sense of otherness is what had covered Her nakedness. It's Her dress. That's why She's called "Brahmamayi." It means that Brahman and maya are one. She's formless *and* She has form. When the covering of who you take yourself to be, the personality, is removed, then She stands alone.

So your absence as a person is what makes her presence possible to be revealed. Or is that not necessarily so?

It could be looked at that way, though that's not exactly the way I'd say it.

How would you say it?

She's playing *all* the roles. She puts on the cloth. She takes off the cloth. It has nothing to do with you or your absence or anything else. There was nothing other than Her, all along. You know what I mean?

Beautiful. Thank you.

She's the One that's appearing as you.

Identification Is The Problem – Not The Mind Itself

And that's why the ego sense isn't an obstacle to realization?

The *identification* of Consciousness as being an ego would be an obstacle. The ego's not the obstacle – it's the *identification*. Identification with the ego is exclusiveness and non-identification with the ego is inclusiveness.

So an egoic nature is a limiting sense, a consciousness that excludes everything but itself and says, "I am the ego" whereas, in realization, consciousness includes the totality, including the ego. Expands to include.

That would be a better way of looking at it. Yes. It's *identifications* that give rise to the problem, not the things.

So identifying with an activity.

Identification with the ego and all its needs chain a person, because they feel deficient within themselves and believe they need things in order to be happy. Then, if these things are removed or compromised, they're not happy. They're dependent on things for their happiness, which creates a sense of need, a sense of perpetually needing something from the outside, needing things to go a certain way in order to be happy.

But those things *in themselves* aren't the obstacles. The obstacle is the way that you look at them with your sense of need. I mean, the underlying Awareness remains the same. It can stand revealed, whether you're rich, poor, have sex, have no sex, or whatever. Reality still exists, you know? You still have an inner Self – no matter what.

An inner self, as in The inner Self?

Yes. It's always there. If you eat a piece of apple pie and you experience joy, the joy's coming from the Self, it's not coming from the pie. The pie is an occasion that puts the mind in a disposition that allows the Self to flash forth from within. The Self is always there. But the maya is that one doesn't realize that the joy is coming from within. Very few understand that, even when you're having a cup of tea, the joy isn't coming from the tea – the joy is coming from the Self. People touch the Self all the time. Any time you experience joy or happiness, you're touching the Self. Life's an occasion. The big question is: *Is it a conscious occasion or an unconscious occasion?* Because, if you're dependent on a situation to experience the Self, then life has become your cage and you're trapped in nature and circumstance. If you experience the Self directly and radiate that into your situations – where your experience isn't dependent on the nature of the situation – then you're free.

Everything Springs From The One

Thank you. You have said that God doesn't reveal Itself through any teaching or practice, that God simply reveals Itself.

That means that the realization doesn't come *through* anything, because that would give the impression that the realisation, the Self-revealing process, is dependent on something. The Self-revealing process isn't *dependent* on anything.

It's an extension of what we were just saying, in a way.

God stands revealed, but It isn't revealed *through* anything. There's a difference. In other words, the thing comes from grace – grace doesn't come from the thing. The situation springs from grace – grace doesn't spring from the situation.

So the fact, then, that I would choose to engage in meditation or chanting...

You *think* you're choosing. In reality, you *are* choosing, but at the same time, it's the One that's desiring to experience Itself that gives rise to the sense, in you, of wanting to meditate. So the big question is: *Are you the one who's instigating the idea that you want to meditate, or is the Self?* Part of the Self-revealing process is for the desire for meditation to arise. What came first, the chicken or the egg? In our way of looking at things, when the One appears as an individual and then manifests as the desire to merge back into Itself, the Self-revealing process *displays* Itself as one's interest in meditation.

So that's grace – the interest and the choice to meditate.

Grace gives rise to the interest in the first place. It's not that grace comes from the interest; the interest is due to grace. We put everything back to the One, you see. Everything springs from the One. The One appears as the veil and then the One also appears as knowledge. It plays *all* the roles. *There is no other.* No other player. No other factor. No other thing. You know what I mean?

Yeah.

There is only That.

There's no other thing?

In all these guises, in all these realities, in all these perceptions.

Period. Absolutely.

Absolutely. And in Integral Advaitism, the Self is not just formless, It also appears in these guises. The Self and the Power of Self are one. There is only Consciousness.

And it seems that in this approach – the path of integral Advaita, as you express it – it's important to understand that it's the Self, it's the formless, it's the whole universe, and the power of grace functions through the practices and the teachings, the environment of worship, and the sacred spaces. That seems to be an important distinction as I am understanding it.

Well, an awakening could come through anything. However, in the same way that certain foods have been demonstrated as being good for your body, certain situations are conducive to the Self-revealing process. So, if one's attracted to those situations, it shows that grace is at work. But the big question is: *Is grace at work because you're interested in these situations, or is your interest in these situations due to grace?* We would say you're interested in these situations due to grace, you see, because it always goes back to the greater Reality.

The greater power.

Yes. That which gives rise to all these gradations of awareness.

Brilliant. So how do you feel about what we've covered?

I like it. Why not? What else would happen?

Well, thank you.

Conclusion:
Classical Teachings On The Nature Of Kundalini

Kundalini: Her Three Aspects
By Swami Shankaracharya

Kundalini's one, however when functioning in different ways She's known by different names.

Prana Kundalini
Prana Kundalini is the aspect of Goddess Kundalini which supports the pranic functions of the body. She's the energy of ones biological existence, as well as the link between the mental and physical realms. Ones spiritual endeavors, as well as the blessings of Shaktipat, all bear fruit through Her grace.

When awakened, Prana Kundalini sends out emanations from muladhar which energize and enliven the entire pranic system. Then working as the enlivened pranas, She brings about the necessary purification's paving the way for Her own grand ascent. During this ascent, She vibrates the chakras and absorbs their energies and qualities into Her upward flow.
At ajna chakra, She automatically manifests as Chit Kundalini, granting spiritual knowledge and then in sahasrar merges with Siva as Para Kundalini. Prana Kundalinis known to grant both bhukti and mukti, worldly enjoyment and liberation. This is the most common type of ascent.

Attitudes and practices emphasizing purification of body, mind and soul, as well as the importance of invoking and serving God in the world draw a response from Prana Kundalini.

Chit Kundalini

Chit Kundalini is the aspect of Goddess Kundalini which supports psychological function. Mental and emotional processes yield spiritual fruit through Her blessings.

Unlike Prana Kundalini, Chit Kundalinis activities are not experienced as movements of energy, but rather as expansion of awareness. During Her ascent She flashes quickly to ajna or above, without vibrating the chakras or absorbing their energies and qualities. She's known to grant mukti - the bliss of liberation, however is not associated with granting bhukti - the unique enjoyment made possible by this absorption. Although Chit Kundalinis heightened activities (in muladhar) may grant deep spiritual insight and lofty states of awareness, these activities do not directly purify the energy system (as do those of Prana Kundalini). Without this advantage, Her full ascent (from muladhar) and consequent realization based on ones own ability and power of practice is rare.

Intellectual approaches such as jnana yoga, emphasizing Self inquiry, detachment and similar practices draw a response from Chit Kundalini.

Para Kundalini

Para Kundalini is undifferentiated and supreme. She stands alone, upholding the entire universe.

Note: One may worship the Divine Mother as the transcendental Reality and at the same time disassociate themself from Her Energy and Its manifestations. In such a case, even though the Divine Mother is worshiped, She may awaken as Chit Kundalini. Or, there's the possibility that one may invoke the Energy of Kundalini and follow the path of jnana yoga as well. This type of approach could draw a response from both Prana Kundalini and Chit Kundalini. Shri Kundalini may work in purifying the energy system as Prana Kundalini and simultaneously radiate influences supporting the intellectual processes of recognition, as Chit Kundalini (from muladhar). The possibilities are endless.

Common Misconceptions
By Swami Shankaracharya

There's a common belief among many following the path of knowledge (jnanis) that awakening of Kundalini is unnecessary and realization takes place in the heart rather than in sahasrar.

While jnanis generally associate spiritual progress with a descent of awareness into the heart, integral yogis recognize that through Self inquiry prana becomes concentrated in the heart which in turn vibrates the sushumna causing Chit Kundalini to Flash forth giving rise to their experience.

Since Chit Kundalini does not display Herself as movement, some erroneously conclude that Kundalini's not involved. It's important to note that Prana Kundalini, which is experienced rising through the chakras, upon reaching ajna automatically becomes Chit Kundalini and then mirrors the same states as those experienced by the jnanis during their decent into the heart. This is because they are the same. There's no jnana without the awakening and unfolding of Chit Kundalini.

In regards to the idea that liberation takes place in the heart rather than sahasrar. The integral way of saying this would be that the awareness of sahasrar must be brought to the heart. After experiencing union in sahasrar Kundalini is not able to stay in the higher realms and often returns to muladhar. This is because even though certain tendencies were transcended during Her ascent, their limiting constructs still exist. When Kundalini is firmly established in sahasrar She will naturally return to the heart (or above). When the awareness of sahasrar is brought to the heart (the pranic center of the body), not only is the binding effect of karmic limitations rendered ineffective, but all is seen as Consciousness. This is true liberation!

Some teach that the path of Self inquiry is the direct path and therefore there's no need to worry about the chakras or Kundalini. The role of Chit Kundalini has already been pointed out. Also, the direct path is the one that works. A full unfolding of Chit Kundalini based on ones own power of Self inquiry and detachment is extremely rare. The much easier path is the arousal of Prana Kundalini which automatically leads to the manifestation of Chit Kundalini and true jnana, the goal of Self inquiry.

Integral Yoga maintains that the highest goal of life is not simply the attainment of mukti or transcendental freedom, but also bhukti or free participation in the creative joy of the Spirit.

It is not enough to attain self-realisation ; there is a much nobler goal of human effort, and that is to achieve self-manifestation, i.e., to bring out into the world of Nature the glories of self-realisation. It is not enough to effect complete liberation from Nature ; there is a much sublimer goal of human effort, and that is to live a life of divine activity after the attainment of individual liberation, so that Nature herself can be assisted in her liberation, that is, in the complete fruition of the creative urge concealed in her bosom. Those who are enamoured of the ideal of mukti pursue a path of negation, the via negativa of Christian mystics; they choose to rise higher and higher until the highest point is reached from which there is no coming back.

Integral yoga, however, emphasises the necessity of supplementing ascent by descent, negation by a deeper and fuller affirmation.

One has surely first of all to climb the path of ascent and shoot up to the loftiest summit of spiritual experience. But if one is to participate in the creative joy of the Spirit, one has got to know how to correlate the upward movement of human aspiration with the downward movement of the dynamic Divine.

Having reached the pinnacle of supramental realisation, the integral yogin is again to descend; he is to come back to the point of his departure, namely, to the physical consciousness, and he is to bring down there the light and power of the supramental Truth-Conciousness.

The aim of the integral yogin is to make the supermind overtly operative in our life and to make it a permanent ingredient in the earth-consciousness. Ascent and descent are then two inseparable aspects of the movement of integral yoga ; they are the systol and diastole of integral sadhana. "Our yoga", says Sri Aurobindo, "is a double movement of ascent and descent; one rises to higher and higher levels of consciousness, but at the same time one brings down their power not only into mind and life, but in the end even into the body. And the highest of these levels, the one at which it aims is the Supermind. Only when that can be brought down is a divine trans-formation possible in the earth-consciousness."

> I see the Goddess of Tripura who lives in the Srichakra,
> Who tells me that , Oh son I am pleased with you,
> Because of your chanting daily the holy sound "Hreem",
> And having traveled in the broad unified path of yogis.

Stepping still further into the realm of pure Shakta , the "Devi Mahatmyam" unequivocally states that She *is* the Supreme Brahman -- the entire Shakti-Shiva unity being itself a lesser tattva. She is the Ocean; all other conceptions and manifestations of God or Goddess are merely waves upon that Ocean.

Glossary

Abhinavagupta   (approx. 950–1020 AD) Was one of India's greatest philosophers and mystics. He was considered an important musician, poet, dramatist, theologian and was one of the central figures of non-dual Kashmir Shaivism.

Absolute   The highest Reality; supreme Consciousness; the pure, untainted, changeless Truth.

Acharya   A guide or instructor in religious matters; founder, or leader of a sect.

Adept   An individual identified as having attained a specific level of knowledge, skill, or aptitude.

Adi Parashakti   The original, primordial, vast, womb-energy of the universe.

Adi Shankara   (788 CE–820 CE) Was an Indian philosopher who consolidated the doctrine of Advaita Vedanta, a sub-school of Vedanta. His teachings are based on the unity of the soul and Brahman (God) According to Adi Shankara, God, the Supreme Cosmic Spirit or Brahman is the One, the whole and the only reality. His philosophy is succinctly summarised in the following statement: "Brahman is the only truth, the world is an illusion, and there is ultimately no difference between Brahman and individual self."

Advaita   Literally meaning, not two, non-duality.

Aham Bhramasmi   Vedic mantra, I am Brahman (God.)

Ajana Ignorance (of one's true nature.)

Ajna Chakra The eye which sees inwardly; the "third eye;" the cranial chakra which "sees" in meditation. See also Chakra.

Amrita Nadi Sanskrit for Channel (or Current, or Nerve) of Ambrosia (or Immortal Nectar).

Amrita Sahaja Samadhi Abiding effortlessly as nectar-like Pure Consciousness.

Amrita That which is immortal. Nectar of the Gods. Also refers to the divine nectar that flows down from the sahasrara chakra when the Kundalini is awakened.

Ananda Bliss or Joy.

Anandamayi Ma (1896–1982) A Hindu spiritual teacher and guru from Bengal considered a saint and hailed as one of the prominent mystics of the 20th century. Anandamayi Ma was considered by many to be an Avatar of the Divine Mother.

Anatman Non-self, the absence of self.

Anusthan Referring to spiritual practices performed with dedication for a set period.

Apparition Referring to a perceivable, although non-physical manifestation of a supernatural or spiritual presence.

Arati A ritual act of worship during which a flame, symbolic of the individual soul, is waved before the form of a deity, enlightened being, or an image that represents the light of Consciousness.

Asana Posture or manner of sitting (as in the practice of yoga).

Ashram A hermitage or place of disciplined spiritual retreat.

Atma vichara Enquiry into the nature of the Self.

Atman A Sanskrit word that means "self."

Aum (OM) The primal sound or vibration from which the universe emanates.

Aurobindo (1872–1950) An Indian philosopher, yogi, guru, and poet. The central theme of his vision was the evolution of human life into life divine. He asserts "Man is a transitional being. He is not final. The step from man to superman is the next approaching achievement in the earth evolution. It is inevitable because it is at once the intention of the inner spirit and the logic of nature's process."

Austerities Disciplined spiritual practices. See also Sadhana.

Avatar An incarnation of the Divine in human or animal form.

Baba Father, also a term of affection for an elderly person or saint.

Bhagavan The blessed Lord, the blessed One.

Bhakti Devotion to God.

Bhandas Body locks or muscular contractions applied for the retention and channeling of Kundalini energy.

Bhava The Sanskrit word for "feeling," "emotion," "mood" or "devotional state of mind."

Bija Mantra A Bija mantra is a sacred vowel, which when intoned, resonates with a specific aspect of the Divine. Bija means seed. A Bija Mantra is a seed sound. Each chakra has its own Bija-Mantra. There is no Bija mantra for the Crown Chakra (Sahasrara.) See list of Chakra Bija mantras below.

- Third eye Chakra (Ajna.) AUM
- Throat Chakra (Vishuddha.) HAM
- Heart Chakra (Anahata.) YAM
- Navel Chakra (Manipura.) RAM
- Sacral Chakra (Savadhisthana.) VAM
- Base Chakra (Muladhara.) LAM

Bindu The point without a center from which proceeds Cosmic Sound. Also known as neela bindu, the blue dot, or the blue pearl. The Bindu is said to be a kind of window between the manifest and unmanifest realms, through which the energy of pure potentiality flows into the manifest world.

Bodhisattva A being who, having developed the Awakening Mind (a mind infused with the aspiration to attain the state of enlightenment,) devotes his or her life to the task of achieving enlightenment for the sake of all beings.

Brahman In Vedic philosophy, the absolute Reality. The eternal, unchanging, infinite, immanent, and transcendent reality which is the Divine Ground of all matter, energy, time, space, being, and everything beyond in this Universe. The nature of Brahman is described as transpersonal, personal and impersonal.

Buddhi Discerning, discriminating aspect of mind; from the root "bodh," "to be aware of," "to know;" the intellect. Considered the higher mind, spiritual intuition, or one's capacity for higher reasoning.

Castenada, Carlos Author of a series of books narrating in first person purported experiences under the tutelage of a Yaqui "Man of Knowledge" named Don Juan Matus.

Chakra Literally means "wheels" within the subtle body, which distribute the flow of Shakti, the force of life/feeling/energy. The subtle body is said to have seven chakras, extending from the muladhara at the base of the spine to the sahasrara in the crown of the head.

Chit (Chitti) Consciousness.

Christ Consciousness The consciousness or awareness of the all pervading presence of God, both within oneself and within the totality of manifestation.

Crazy wisdom Refers to an unconventional form of spiritual instruction in which a spiritual master uses any and all means to instruct a disciple experientially in spiritual principles.

Darshan Literally meaning "vision" to glimpse; to see; to have a vision of God.

Data Concepts, ideas.

Deity A deity is a supernatural immortal being, who may be thought of as holy, divine, or sacred, held in high regard, often religiously referred to as a god.

Devi Female deity; goddess.

Devi bhavas Rare spontaneous manifestations of the Divine Mother, which arise in meditation. The Divine Mother manifesting Herself through the vehicle of a spiritual aspirant.

Dharma That which upholds or supports, generally translated into English as "law." It can also mean Duty or what is required to be done. Dharma is akin to the word Law in the sense Jesus used the word, as in the underlying spiritual Law of life. The antonym of dharma is adharma meaning unnatural or immoral.

Dhyana Meditation.

Dhyanyogi Madhusudandas (1878–1994) A great Kundalini Yoga Master, Dhyanyogi emanated an amazingly intense and extraordinary shakti energy field.

Diksha Spiritual Initiation.

Divine Mother The Goddess, the feminine aspect of the Divine, Shakti. God in action.

Durga The warrior aspect of the Divine Mother. Durga is a form of Devi, the supremely radiant goddess, depicted as having ten arms, riding a lion or a tiger, carrying weapons and a lotus flower, maintaining a meditative smile, and practising mudras, or symbolic hand gestures.

Empowerment The process of energy transfer wherein an aspirant's subtle energy system is infused with spiritual energy in the presence of an accomplished spiritual teacher. See also Shakti Pat.

Energetic balancing Refers to various holistic therapeutic processes designed to balance the human energy system.

Energetic phenomena Refers to the various manifestations of awakened spiritual energy (Kundalini) such as spontaneous yogic movements, healings, visions, Divine lights or sounds etc, which may arise during the process of spiritual awakening.

Enlightenment The discovery of one's true nature, traditionally considered the final attainment on the spiritual path, when the limited sense of "I" dissolves revealing the splendour of Consciousness.

Godavri Ma (1914–1991) Female saint/sage from India.

Gurdjieff (1866–1949) Was a mystic and spiritual teacher. He called his discipline "The Work" (connoting "work on oneself") or (originally) the "Fourth Way." At one point he described his teaching as "esoteric Christianity."

Guru Spiritual teacher or Master, one who removes ignorance or darkness by bestowing light.

Guru Maharaj Also known as Prem Pal Singh Rawat, is an Indian Guru who teaches a meditation practice he calls Knowledge. At the age of eight, he succeeded his father Hans Ji Maharaj as leader of the Divine Light Mission.

Guru principle The all pervading power of grace present as the inner Self of all beings.

Gururupayah Meaning the "Guru is the means" (to liberation.)

High tech meditation Referring to a form of meditation developed by Master Charles Cannon, which utilizes music and sound technology to entrain whole brain synchrony.

Holism (From holos, a Greek word meaning all, whole, entire, total) Is the idea that all the properties of a given system (physical, biological, chemical, social, economic, mental, linguistic, etc.) cannot be determined or explained by its component parts alone. Instead, the system as a whole determines in an important way how the parts behave.

Ichazo, Oscar (Born 1931) is the Bolivian-born founder of the Arica School which he established in 1968. Ichazo's teachings are designed to help people transcend their identification with (and the suffering caused by) their own mechanistic thought and behaviour patterns.

Jiddu Krishnamurti (1895–1986) An enlightened writer and speaker on philosophical, social and spiritual issues. His subject matter included psychological revolution, the nature of the mind, meditation, human relationships, and bringing about positive change in society.

Jiva The self, soul, or individual consciousness.

Jnana Knowledge (of one's true nature.)

Jnana yoga Yoga of knowledge and wisdom attained through self-enquiry and self-investigation.

Joy, Brugh (1939–2009) An American spiritual teacher of heart-centered transformation and spiritual enlightenment.

Kali The Hindu goddess associated with eternal energy, time and death. The name Kali comes from kāla, which means black. Kali is represented with perhaps the fiercest features amongst all the world's deities. She has four arms, with a sword in one hand and the head of a demon in another. The other two hands bless her worshippers, and say, "fear not!" She has two dead heads for her earrings, a string of skulls as necklace, and a girdle made of human hands as her clothing. Her tongue protrudes from her mouth, her eyes are red, and her face and breasts are sullied with blood. She stands with one foot on the thigh, and another on the chest of her husband, Shiva.

Kalki Avatar In Hinduism, Kalki is the tenth and final Maha Avatar (great incarnation) of Vishnu who will come to end the present age of darkness and destruction known as Kali Yuga.

Karma Action, "Results of doing." The inevitable law of cause and effect.

Karma yoga Yoga of action; action performed with meditative awareness; action in which the fruits of the action are surrendered to God, yoga of dynamic meditation.

Kashmir Shaivism A Hindu philosophy of Nonduality which arose in Kashmir and made significant strides, both philosophical and theological, until the end of the twelfth century CE. Kashmir Shaivism asserts that Chitti (consciousness) is the one reality. Matter is not separated from consciousness, but rather identical to it. There is no gap between God and the world. The world is not an illusion (as in Advaita Vedanta,) rather the perception of duality is the illusion.

Kriya Literally meaning "action" used to denote spontaneous yogic movements which arise as a result of the activity of awakened spiritual energy (Kundalini) which are purifactory in nature, removing blockages in the subtle energy system.

Kundalini Literally meaning "coiled." Known as the "serpent power;" spiritual energy or evolutionary potential within a human being. Kundalini is the infinite creative energy of God. Classically viewed as being coiled at the base of the human spine in the muladara (root) chakra. Traditionally said to rise up in spiritual awakening from the base of the spine to the crown of the head, piercing all seven chakras in its wake, finally merging with God in the crown of the head (Sahasara.)

Kundalini Maha yoga A name for Kundalini Yoga meaning the Great Yoga.

Kundalini yoga A Path of yoga, which awakens the dormant spiritual energy or force.

Lakshmi Aspect of the Goddess Consciousness manifesting as wealth and abundance. The consort of Vishnu.

Lila Play or Sport. God's play as the universe; the totality of manifestation viewed as inherently Self-arising; the uncaused, unceasing, spontaneously-arising activity of the One Universal Consciousness.

Lokas Planes of consciousness inhabited by sentient beings.

Maha Samadhi Final liberation experienced on the departure of the spirit from the body.

Mantra A sound, syllable, word, or group of words that are considered capable of creating spiritual transformation.

Maya The veiling power of the Divine Mother. Also meaning illusion; partial understanding; wrong or false notions about self-identity.

Meister Eckhart (c. 1260 – c. 1327) was a German theologian, philosopher and mystic.

Merrell-Wolff, Franklin (1887–1985) An American mystical philosopher.

Mudra Psychic gesture; psycho physiological posture, movement or attitude, symbolic hand gestures.

Nadis Invisible conduits of psychic energy, woven throughout the subtle body. Most authorities say there are 72,000 of them.

Navratri A Hindu festival of worship of Shakti. The word Navaratri literally means nine nights in Sanskrit. During these nine nights and ten days, nine forms of Shakti/Devi are worshiped.

Nirvana Final emancipation. Nirvana means extinction, also used to indicate final enlightenment (extinction of ego) and the realm of Infinite unchanging reality.

Nirvikalpa Samadhi Formless absorption. A state of absorption in God where the soul realizes itself and the Eternal Spirit of all that is as essentially and fundamentally one. The most profound meditative transcendence of the mind into its most prior, formless, Self Awareness.

Nisargadatta Maharaj (1897–1981) One of the 20th century's most famous exponents of the school of Advaita Vedanta philosophy (nondualism,) Sri Nisargadatta, was known for his direct and minimalistic expression of nonduality.

Nityananda, Bhagawan (1897–1961) A Hindu Avatar and powerful shaktipat guru. His teachings are published in the "Chidakash Gita." He was the spiritual master of Baba Muktananda.

Nonduality Not two. State of oneness with all. See also Advaita.

Noumenal Energy The all pervading energy of spirit, which acts as a bridge between the manifest and unmanifest realms.

Noumenon Refers to the Unmanifest realm of pure potentiality, that which is not a "thing," not an "object" of the senses. Pure Subjectivity.

Parabhakti Supreme Devotion.

Paramahansa Ramakrishna (1836–1886) A famous God intoxicated mystic of 19th-century India. He was a priest of the Dakshineswar Kali Temple, dedicated to the goddess Kali. Many of his disciples and devotees believe he was an avatar or incarnation of God. His first spiritual teacher was an ascetic woman skilled in both Tantra and Bhakti yoga. Later an advaita teacher taught him non-dual meditation, and according to Ramakrishna, he experienced nirvikalpa samadhi under his guidance. Ramakrishna also experimented with other religions, notably Islam and Christianity, and said that they all lead to the same God.

Paramatman The Supreme Self.

Parasamvit The unbroken experience of supreme oneness.

Parashakti The Supreme, Primordial Energy of the Universe.

Patanjali The compiler of the Yoga Sutras, an important collection of aphorisms on Yoga practice.

Prana Vital energy; inherent vital force pervading every dimension of matter, breath, life, light, universal energy.

Pranayama A Sanskrit word meaning "restraint of the prana or breath." The word is composed of two Sanskrit words, Prāna, life force, or vital energy, particularly, the breath, and "āyāma," to suspend or restrain. It is often translated as control of the life force.

Puranas "of ancient times" are a genre of important Hindu, Jain and Buddhist religious texts, notably consisting of narratives of the history of the universe from creation to destruction, genealogies of kings, heroes, sages, and demigods, and descriptions of Hindu cosmology, philosophy, and geography.

Raja Yoga "Royal yoga," "royal union," also known as Classical Yoga. Raja Yoga is concerned principally with the cultivation of the mind using meditation.

Rakshasa A race of mythological humanoid beings or demons in Hindu and Buddhist mythology

Ramana Maharshi (1879–1950) An Indian sage who attained liberation at the age of 16. After which he left home for Arunachala, a mountain considered sacred by Hindus and lived there for the rest of his life. He popularized the spiritual practice known as self inquiry.

Ramesh Moudgil A Tantric master and Shakta adept from India.

Rig Veda An ancient Indian sacred collection of Vedic Sanskrit hymns.

Rishi Seer; realized sage; one who contemplates or meditates on the Self.

Rudra A name of Shiva. Rudra and Shiva are viewed as being the same personality in a number of Hindu traditions. Rudra, the god of the roaring storm, is usually portrayed in accordance with the element he represents as a fierce, destructive deity.

Sadhana "Direct way." A spiritual ritual, or spiritual discipline.

Sadhu A holy person or a person who has renounced the world for God.

Sahaja Spontaneous, easy, natural, effortless.

Sahaja Samadhi Spontaneous meditative absorption, where the mind is effortlessly withdrawn from the external world and fully dissolved in the Self or God.

Sahasrara Chakra The "wheel" of spiritual energy which opens into complete and total self-transcendence or God realisation at the top of the head. Also known as the crown chakra or the thousand petalled lotus. See also Chakra.

Samadhi Complete absorption in the object of one's contemplation. Meditative absorption in the Self.

Samsara The phenomenal, perceptible world; which can be tasted, touched, seen, heard, or smelled. The ever changing world of birth, death and rebirth.

Samskaras A collection impressions stored deep within the mind. See also Vasanas.

Sannyas Renunciation of the world to pursue a deeper relationship with God. Monkhood, also the ceremony and vows of monkhood.

Sannyasin Monk, one who is devoted to a life of spiritual growth and service to others.

Sanskrit "Language of the gods," original Vedic language.

Saraswati The goddess of knowledge, music and the arts.

Sat Existence or being, reality, truth.

Satori A Japanese Buddhist term for enlightenment that literally means "understanding." In the Zen Buddhist tradition, satori refers to a flash of sudden awareness, Satori is typically juxtaposed with the related term kensho, which translates as "seeing one's nature."

Satsang Association with Truth, a spiritual gathering in which the ideals and principles of truth are discussed.

Shakta Adept One who has gained a high level of mastery in the formal practices of worship of the various manifestations of Shakti in the form of Kali, Saraswati, Durga, etc.

Shakti The Primordial energy of Consciousness, the Energy or Power of God. The Feminine counterpart to the Supreme Lord, Shiva. Shiva Shakti is God.

Shaktipat Literally "energy transfer," also meaning descent of grace. A process akin to one candle lighting another, shaktipat is an infusion of spiritual energy from teacher to student, which sparks or ignites the Kundalini process in the recipient. See also empowerment.

Shiva Literally meaning "auspicious one" Shiva is a name for the All-pervading Reality, "Sat Chit Ananda"(truth, consciousness, bliss.) Shiva is also seen as that Ultimate Reality embodied as the supreme Lord of the Universe in the form of the Original Primordial Yogi, Lord Shiva.

Shiva Sutra's The foundational scripture of Kashmir Shaivism, attributed to the divine revelations of the sage Vasugupta.

Siddha A fully Self-realized yogi.

Siddha Loka A spiritual plan of existence.

Soma See Amrita.

Spanda Meaning "slight movement," "oscillation," "vibration" or "quivering." Referring to the primal creative impulse of God.

Sri Term of respect and a title of veneration for deities (usually translated as "Lord.")

St John of the Cross (1542–1591) A Spanish mystic, Catholic saint, Carmelite friar and priest, his inspired mystical writings reflect the universal nature of spiritual awakening.

St Teresa of Avila (1515–1582) Was a prominent Spanish mystic, Roman Catholic saint, Carmelite nun, writer and theologian of contemplative life through mental prayer. She was a reformer of the Carmelite Order and is considered to be, along with John of the Cross, a founder of the Discalced Carmelites. An account of her inner life and her writings on the nature of prayer can be found in her book "The Interior Castle."

Subtle body The second of four bodies within a human being (the physical, subtle, causal, and supra-causal bodies.) The subtle body is connected with the dream state, the causal body is connected with deep sleep and the supra-causal body is associated with pure consciousness or transcendent awareness.

Subtle dimensions Referring to the subtle, causal and supra-causal dimensions of Life beyond the physical.

Sunyata Emptiness, the void, the abyss.

Sushumna Central nadi or channel in the spine, which conducts the Kundalini or spiritual force from the muladhara (base chakra) to sahasrara (crown chakra.)

Sutra An aphorism.

Swami Muktananda (1908–1982) Also known as Baba. An Indian Kundalini Yoga Master and powerful Shakti Pat Guru who travelled extensively in the West. A disciple of Bhagavan Nityananda.

Tantra Meaning wide-ranging, whole. It also evokes the weave of a fabric. The word Tantra generally refers to the scriptures called "Tantras" which are commonly identified with the worship of Shakti. Tantra deals primarily with spiritual practices and ritual forms of worship, which aim at liberation from ignorance and rebirth, the universe being regarded as the divine play of Shakti and Shiva.

Tao (Way.) The Unchanging principle behind the universe; the primordial source of all that is. The Tao-te Ching describes it as "something formlessly fashioned, that existed before Heaven and Earth." Sometimes described more loosely as "doctrine" or "principle," it is generally used to signify the primordial essence or fundamental aspect of the universe.

Tao-te Ching (Book of the Way and its Power.) Foundational text of Taoism. Attributed to Lao-tzu and probably composed in the 4th century BCE, it teaches about the Tao.

Taoism Refers to a variety of philosophical traditions and related spiritual practices that have influenced Eastern Asia for more than two millennia. The Three Jewels of the Tao are compassion, moderation, and humility. Taoist thought emphasizes nature and the relationship between humanity and the cosmos.

Taoist A practitioner of Taoism.

Transcendental Consciousness The All-pervading, universal Consciousness both within and beyond manifestation.

Upanishads Philosophical texts considered to be an early source of Hindu religion. The inspired teachings, visions, and mystical experiences of the ancient sages (rishis) of India.

Vasanas The impressions remaining in the mind, the present consciousness of past (life) perceptions, knowledge derived from memory. Hence vasanas are preconscious inclinations that create the structure and functioning of the mind; deeply rooted habit patterns or psychological tendencies that go on to form conscious desires and actions. See also Samskaras.

Vedanta Originally a word used in Hindu philosophy as a synonym for that part of the Veda texts known also as the Upanishads. The word is also used to describe the group of philosophical Hindu traditions concerned with the self-realisation by which one understands the ultimate nature of reality Beyond all knowledge; transcendental wisdom.

Vedas From the Sanskrit word veda meaning "knowledge." A large body of texts originating in ancient India, composed in Vedic Sanskrit. The texts constitute the oldest layer of Sanskrit literature and the oldest scriptures of Hinduism.

Vedic Referring to the Vedas, the oldest preserved Indic texts.

Vimarsha The "reflection" of pure awareness in the world of phenomena, bodily and mental, inner and outer, that are its own expression or manifestation. The self reflective power in Consciousness.

Vipassana In the Buddhist tradition Vipassana means insight into the nature of reality, it is a practice of self-transformation through self-observation and introspection.

Vishnu A Hindu name for God. Vishnu is the ultimate omnipresent reality.

Vortices See chakras.

Whole brain synchrony Refers to the balance of the left and right hemispheres of the brain, which occurs in deep meditation.

Yajna The word yajna comes from the root – "yaj" which means to worship. The closest single English word for yajna is sacrifice. A Yajna is the act of sacrifice/offering/worshiping. In the general sense it can be understood as any action done with the sense of sacrifice, like praying, remembering, meditating.

Yoga From the root yuj (to "yoke," "join" or "unite"). Meaning both Union; union with the Absolute and also the means to attain that unity (of the individual soul with the universal awareness or God.)

Yoga sutras A Hindu scripture and foundational text of Yoga.

Yogi A practitioner of Yoga

Zen A school of Buddhism. The word Zen is from the Japanese pronunciation of the Chinese word Chan, which in turn is derived from the Sanskrit word dhyana, which means "meditation" or "meditative state." The establishment of Zen is credited to the monk Bodhidharma, who came to China to teach a "special transmission outside scriptures, not founded on words or letters."

Suggested Reading

Bentov, Itzhak. 1977, *Stalking The Wild Pendulum: On The Mechanics Of Consciousness*, Destiny Books, Vermont

Brinton Perrera, Sylvia. 1981, *Descent To The Goddess; A Way Of Initiation For Women*, Inner City Books, Canada

Cannon, Master Charles. 2015 *Forgiving the Unforgivable: The True Story of How Survivors of the Mumbai Terrorist Attack Answered Hatred with Compassion: The Power of Holistic Living* . Tandava Press, Australia

Cannon, Master Charles. 1997, *The Bliss Of Freedom; A Contemporary Mystic's Enlightening Journey*, Acacia Publishing Company, USA

Cannon, Master Charles. 2002, *The Synchronicity Experience; Practical Spirituality…Holistic Lifestyle*, The Synchronicity Foundation International, Nellysford

Conway, Timothy. 1996, *Women of Power and Grace: Nine Astonishing, Inspiring Luminaries of Our Time*, Wake Up Press, California

Emoto, Masaru. 2004, *The Hidden Messages In Water*, Beyond Words Publishing, Oregon

Frawley, David. 2008, *Inner Tantric Yoga: Working with the Universal Shakti: Secrets of Mantras, Deities, and Meditation*, Lotus Press, India

Harding, Elizabeth U. 1993, *Kali: The Black Goddess Of Dakshineswar*, Nicolas-Hays, Inc. USA

Johnsen, Linda. 1994, *Daughters of the Goddess: The Women Saints of India*, Yes International Publishers, Minnesota

LaRue, Ronda. 2003, *Remembering Who You Really Are: The Journey Of Awakening To Soul*, IUniverse, USA

Merell-Wolff, Franklin. 1983, *Pathways Through To Space*, Julian Press, New York

Merell-Wolff, Franklin. 1983, *Philosophy of Consciousness Without An Object: Reflections on the Nature of Transcendental Consciousness*, Julian Press, New York

Moss, Richard. 1981, *The I That Is We: Awakening To Higher Energies Through Unconditional Love*, Celestial Arts, California

Moss, Richard. 1987, *The Black Butterfly: An Invitation To Radical Aliveness*, Celestial Arts, California

Moss, Richard. 1995, *The Second Miracle; Intimacy Spiritually And Conscious Relationships*, Celestial Arts, California

Moss, Richard. 1997, *Words That Shine Both Ways*, Enneas Publications, USA

Moss, Richard. 2007, *The Mandala Of Being: Discovering The Power Of Awareness*, New Word Library, California

Moss, Richard. 2011, *Inside-Out Healing: Transforming Your Life Through The Power Of Presence*, Hay House INC. USA

Nityananda. 1981, *Chidakash Geetha*, Eden Books, UK

Patanjali & Hartranft, Chip. 2003, *The Yoga-Sutra of Patanjali: A New Translation with Commentary*, Shambhala Publications Inc. USA

Ramakrishna. 1942, *The Gospel Of Sri Ramakrishna*, Ramakrishna-Vivekananda Center, New York

Scherr, Kia. 2013, *Pocketbook Of Peace*, One Life Alliance, Nellysford, VA

Shankar Das. 1989, *God Alone Is: Essential Teachings From Talks*, Sadhana Ashram, USA

Shankaracharya. 2001, *Goddess Kundalini*, Sadhana Ashram, USA

Singh, Jaideva. 2005, *Spanda-Karikas: The Divine Creative Pulsation*, Motilal Banarsidass Publishing, New Delhi

Singh, Jaideve. 2000, *Siva Sutras: The Yoga Of Supreme Identity*, Motilal Banarsidass Publishing, New Delhi

Spero, David. 2000, *Beyond The Place Of Laughter And Tears In The Land Of Devotion*, Paramatman Productions, USA

St John of the Cross. 1991, *The Collected Works Of St John Of The Cross*, ICS Publications, Washington, DC

St John of the Cross. 2003, *Dark Night Of The Soul*, Dover Publications, New York

St Teresa of Avila. 2007, *Interior Castle*, Dover Publications, New York

Swami Muktananda. 2000, *The Play Of Consciousness*, SYDA Foundation, US

Contact Information

Swami Shankaracharya
Sadhana Ashram
1408 McAndrew Road Ojai, CA 93023 USA
805.640.1688
sadhanaashram@mindspring.com
www.sadhanaashram.org

David Spero
PO Box 283
Novato, CA 94948-0283
www.davidspero.org

Dr Richard Moss
Richard Moss Seminars
PO Box 1379
Ojai, CA 93024
(800) 647-0755
info@RichardMoss.com
www.richardmoss.com

Master Charles Cannon
Synchronicity Foundation
2610 Adial RD
Faber, VA 22938 USA
757.644.3400 – Toll Free 1.800.962.2033
Fax 434.361.1058
Synch@synchronicity.org
www.synchronicity.org

Kia Scheer
One Life Alliance
2610 Adial Rd
Faber, VA 22938
kiascherr@onelifealliance.org
www.onelifealliance.org

David Rivers
Tandava Press
kundaliniprocess@gmail.com
www.thedanceofkundalini.com
www.tandavapress.com

The Tandava Foundation
foundationtantra@gmail.com
www.tandavafoundation.com

About The Author

David Rivers is a spiritual teacher in a lineage of master spiritual teachers that dates back thousands of years. Anchored in the Tantric philosophical system. His focus includes Kundalini Yoga, Non-Duality and Empowerment. He offers retreats and programs designed to elicit the awakening of the spiritual current.

David Rivers
Tandava Press
kundaliniprocess@gmail.com
www.thedanceofkundalini.com
www.tandavapress.com

The Tandava Foundation

The Tandava Foundation emerged as a natural extension of David's passion for Sacred Activism. The Tandava Foundation aims to engage in meaningful community service work. Such as providing food for those in need. As well as organizing fund raising events, to raise money to be used in charitable projects. Importantly the Tandava Foundation aim's to make spiritual teachings and programs such as meditation classes available in communities stricken by poverty and crime.

The foundation also aims to preserve the foundational texts and scriptures of The Ancient Tantric Tradition. Along with preserving the teachings of authentic western spiritual teachers who embody the Tantric approach. Making these priceless teachings available to those who do not have the means to access them financially is also an aim of the Foundation.

The Tandava Foundation welcomes new members and invites participation from anyone who feels moved to play a role, however large or small in this undertaking. The foundation will provide support and guidance to members who may find themselves inspired to undertake projects aimed at making a difference in the lives of those in genuine need. The Foundation is inherently non-sectarian, its aim is to enrich each whole community, promoting a sense of universal love and compassion. The foundation also aims to provide a comprehensive resource and guidance for people undergoing the Kundalini process.

If you would like to contribute and become a member of the Tandava Foundation and contribute in some way shape or form, please don't hesitate to make contact.

The Tandava Foundation
foundationtantra@gmail.com
www.tandavafoundation.com

www.ingramcontent.com/pod-product-compliance
Lightning Source LLC
Chambersburg PA
CBHW022057160426
43198CB00008B/258